U.S. POLITICS–

Inside and Out

U.S. POLITICS–
Inside and Out

BOOKS by U.S.NEWS & WORLD REPORT

A division of
U.S.News & World Report, Inc., Washington, D.C.

1970

Acknowledgments

Factual material for *Politics—Inside and Out* was gathered first-hand from a number of organizations, public officials, and politicians at all levels of government in many parts of the country.

Among those making special data available were the American Institute of Public Opinion; the American Law Division, Library of Congress; the Committee on Political Education, AFL-CIO; the Democratic National Committee; the Republican National Committee; the Governmental Affairs Institute; the League of Women Voters; the National Association of Counties; the National Council of State Governments; the National Municipal League; the Survey Research Center, University of Michigan; the U.S. Census Bureau; and the U.S. Chamber of Commerce.

Contents

List of Illustrations

PART 1

CHAPTER ONE / **Behind the Scenes**

Does your vote really decide who is to make the laws and run your government? If you think it does, the chances are about 10 to 1 that you are wrong.

Basic decisions are made by a few back-room managers long before an election. When you vote, it is likely that you simply are ratifying the candidates they have selected.

This need not be so, and later chapters indicate how an informed electorate might change matters. But as things stand today, most of us have relatively little to say about the men and women who govern us.

For a better idea of what happens, we might compare government to a large corporation. A relatively small group of men and women, often with large personal investments, can secure control of a major corporation, either publicly or privately owned. Millions of customers of its products or services have little to say about the company's operation.

Similarly, in the case of government, a relatively small group of men and women who invest large amounts of money and time can gain control of the levers of public power. The average citizen is left pretty much in the position of a customer of various public services, such as national defense, police protection, education, and garbage collection, for which he pays with his taxes.

Ninety-seven percent of Americans might be rated as "customers." They give nothing to any political party—no money, no work at the polls, no attendance at precinct meetings, no service as a volunteer worker for any candidate. They sit back, allowing others to get the job done. This leaves the running of government in the hands of 3 percent of the American people.

Like the board of directors of a corporation, the men at the top of this small group make the important decisions about candidates and pass the word down to the rank and file. They represent the large sources of money required for political campaigns of one party or the other at all levels, from county courthouse to statehouse to the White House.

Few politicians can move very far without the word from the money-men. This select group may be composed of as few as a dozen men in each of the 3,043 counties in the United States. As the major "stockholders" in government, they make the basic decisions. They may act in person or work through an agent. Their hand is not always visible. They are labor officials, bankers, industrialists, businessmen, wealthy individuals. Often they hold no political or party office.

Decisions frequently are made privately—at cocktail parties, at small dinners, by telephone, behind the doors of law offices. If there is a meeting of minds on whom to support, things move smoothly. If there is a division of opinion, the state or community may see a struggle for power involving a hot primary campaign.

The men who serve as political agents for the real money-men often turn out to be lawyers. More often than not, they specialize in corporation law and handle the legal affairs of wealthy men, industries, or labor unions. They may be lawyers or lobbyists with a special aptitude for politics. If the latter, they usually are not chosen by the industrialists themselves but by the legal concerns which handle this special aspect of their affairs. The diversion of money into politics is watched carefully to see that there is no crack in the legal ice.

Most every writer on national politics knows many of these political agents, but their names rarely are mentioned in print. To disclose them would destroy an important source of political news.

In several eastern states, the best informed men on politics are the vice presidents of large banks—assigned to watch who is spending the big money on which candidates. In at least three other states, the political experts of oil companies invariably know which way election tides are running. In Montana, you can rely on forecasts of the political manager for mining interests. In Nevada, the operator of a large gambling casino was for many years an unfailing source of information. In at least three states, the best informed sources are labor union officials, and they have an important voice in thirteen others. But in most of the states around the nation, the offices of lawyers for big corporations are the most important ports of call for national political reporters who want to know what is happening behind the scenes of politics.

Many of these men can make predictions with uncanny accuracy. Two political spokesmen for major oil companies have been known to forecast the outcome of as many as thirty congressional races in their states without missing in a single case. In other states, labor officials have been equally accurate. Several spokesmen for labor or business interests in state capitals know the makeup of their state legislatures so well that they can come within one or two votes of knowing in advance the outcome of a test on any piece of legislation in which their groups are interested. This is their business. Moreover, they are watching the action through the windows of the inner sanctum. They work for the big "stockholders" in politics.

When it comes to picking candidates, the men with an important stake in politics start looking over the field early. Often, they will spot a man whose personality and ideas seem to fit their needs five or six years in advance of election to the post they have in mind. They move him up gradually through civic organizations and smaller offices until they decide that the time is right to move him into a more important office.

11

After an agreement among the interested men and groups, candidates are moved forward by state and local politicians. They are put through the party machinery for the official stamp of approval. This is when the voter usually gets a chance to mark his ballot in the primary.

Each party goes through this process, with most of the small "stockholders" endorsing the decisions that already have been made. Some of the large "stockholders" hold "shares" in both political parties. They give money to both sides: By the time the average citizen—in his role of customer—votes in the November general election, he often finds that his choice is limited to two candidates who are remarkably alike.

How to vote in November is a question that rarely troubles people in January, February, and March. The weather often is forbidding. Tax returns have not yet been filed. Farmers are busy with plans for spring planting. City dwellers are preoccupied with their bills. The plans and urgencies of the new year are moving in. Evenings are filled with television, friends, relaxation. It is the basketball season and a time for baseball talk. Teams are heading south for spring training. If ever there is a time when the average citizen's back is turned toward the politicians, this is it.

Yet, winter and early spring are the times when the final choices are being made by the back-room managers. Serious aspirants for offices have been busy for almost a year—sometimes longer—rounding up support, trying to show the coaches that they belong on the team. During the winter, men who hold the political moneybags are studying the records of those who seek office. In small groups or by telephone, candidates and prospects are discussed. At upper levels, there are decisions on whom to support for the United States Senate, the House of Representatives, the governor's mansion, and other statewide offices. Lesser managers of political power in counties and local communities appraise candidates for the state legislature, sheriff's office, county commission, and other local offices.

It is only now and then that a glimpse of this process

emerges to public view. A few years ago, long before the primaries, a member of Congress wrote to a friend that 176 members of the House had benefited from help from labor unions: contributions of money, advisors, advertising, and workers. He wrote:

> Right now in each Congressional district, a half-dozen men in each party are deciding who shall run for Congress. An equal number of businessmen, if they really represented business, in each district could exert a strong influence on this selection and who gets elected.
>
> At present business is so indifferent and so uninformed that few businessmen even know that the next Congress is now being selected. As a result, unqualified men, with anti-business principles, will be elected to get special favors for the special groups who put them in office.

The letter led to a study in depth by the state Chamber of Commerce of the way politics worked in his state. Later, there were broader studies in other states, and the U.S. Chamber of Commerce devised a set of working materials to teach businessmen how to relate themselves to politics.

Knowledgeable political reporters get word of what is happening and write what they can—but carefully. Events are so well hidden that few people have solid information, and these people will not talk for quotation. Small squibs are printed now and then in county and community newspapers. These surface ripples are signs of the scramble among the big fish.

Almost every important politician must turn to the rich men outside politics for the money to finance his campaign. There are more than a dozen states in which it costs over a million dollars to win election as either governor or U.S. senator. Aside from Nelson Rockefeller in New York, Winthrop Rockefeller in Arkansas, and Edward Kennedy in Massachusetts, there are not too many men who can dig into their own pockets for this much money. Most must look elsewhere, whether they are running for a county office or for the presidency.

In a county, the money may come from as few as two or three persons or from a local union. As the officeholder moves up the ladder, however, the group broadens and so does his obligation to the men who provide the money. A senator once said:

> Most of us must depend on friends and interested people for campaign money. We cannot ignore the suggestions of important people after we get in office. The money must come from some place. I wish things were different. But that is the way American politics works. Until we devise some better way of financing compaigns, we have to live with it.

An insight into this side of politics comes from a man who has seen every side of the operation. He is a second generation politician. As a young man, he managed statewide campaigns. He held high offices in his state and is now a U.S. senator. He put it this way:

> Behind every public official, there must be a group of important people. These normally divide into three groups. First are the businessmen who are eager for contracts; they want to sell things to the county, state or whichever branch of government may be involved. Next come the friends of the candidate who really have no demands to make on him. And finally are the people who want power; they want to be big men in their community; they are looking to the future when they may want a judgeship or some other appointment for themselves or their friends; they are on the make and they want to get on the right bandwagon.
>
> The politician deals with different groups when he is running for the Senate from those who have a hand in electing governors. At the Senate level, you are working with spokesmen for union labor, for Negroes and for big

industries. They are interested in favorable legislation, in tax gimmicks, in federal contracts.

At the governorship level, contractors are important. They want to sell road machinery. They want to build highways. They have products that can be used by state hospitals and other institutions. Men who sell the paint used by state hospitals and other institutions. Men who sell the paint used to put lines down the middle of highways have made fortunes. Wholesale liquor dealers are vitally interested in the election of a governor. A man with a $250,000 business may be wiped out by a shift in liquor licenses.

Down at the county level, you always find one, or several, powerful people who must be fitted into any successful campaign. These men may be real estate dealers, farmers, bankers, automobile men, liquor dealers, other business men. They want zoning permits. They want a road across their farm. They want their bank to serve as a redepository for county funds. They want to sell cars to the county. They want liquor licenses, an easement in regulations, all sorts of things.

And remember, always, at every level, there is a constant power struggle between those who are in control and those who want control, between the ins and the outs, between those who have it made and those who are trying to make it. The successful politician must keep these things in mind. He must get the right people in his organization. He must know who is in power and how firmly they are seated at the top of the heap.

Another appraisal came from a state official. This man has served in county government and in the legislature. His family has been involved in local, state, and national politics for several generations. He expressed this view:

There is no single controlling group in my state to dictate who shall run for office. The problem is more tricky. There are many men and groups who are scrambling for power. You have to find the right ones, set your lines early and develop solid support.

We have several wealthy people who are interested in individuals and help to finance their campaigns. These people want nothing from either the state or the individuals whom they support. They are interested in ideas.

Next, we have a group of what might be called "fixers." These are lawyers and others who serve as go-betweens in handling the relations of contractors with state officials. Many of the "fixers" obviously want contracts. But there are others who only want recognition from the people in power. They simply want to feel important.

"Fixers" and fund-raisers often have as much to say about who shall run for office as the titular leaders of political parties. Often, they meet with the politicians in a kind of back-room nominating convention.

Money has become so important to campaigns that politicians are guided in their choice of candidates by the amount of support aspirants for office can win from organized labor, wealthy individuals, and businessmen. Cash often becomes the key to a party nomination. Money must be in hand or nailed down by firm promises. A man who has served both as a big-city mayor and as governor of his state said he never accepted a nomination without knowing exactly where campaign money was coming from. "I want to see the cash on the barrel-head," he said.

Political scientists suggest that money has its greatest effect on political trades before the candidate is chosen. The hold of politicians on the nominating process is being weakened by the substitution of civil service for patronage in hiring employees at many levels of government. This gives men with campaign money a more important voice in picking candidates in maneuvers behind the scenes. Only occasionally does a candidate come along with so much popular support that he can run as a free agent. Usually the back-room managers either get the candidate they want or block the man they do not want until a compromise is reached.

The importance of the managers and fund-raisers in the decision making process cannot be over estimated. A few years ago, an officeholder in California called a meeting of six political associates to decide whether he should try for a higher office. Four of the six men were important fund-raisers. A fifth was the party chairman. The decision was against running that year. He waited until a later campaign and won.

In a rough, off-the-cuff analysis, politicians say that power companies run half a dozen states. Labor unions have the loudest voice in eight or ten others. Three states are dominated by mining interests. Two are lightly influenced by racetrack interests. A cattleman's association has the controlling voice in one state. Oil companies dictate the course of two, and drug and insurance companies can claim another.

Like most generalities, this is not entirely true. Nothing is ever that simple, especially in politics. It takes a combination of interests to win an election in any state, and the people who pull the strings are very quiet about it. They stay far in the background. Many an election has been lost because an opponent turned upon the candidate of "the interests" and accused him of being what he was.

The men who produce large amounts of money, either from their own or from others' pockets, always gain easy access to the officeholders. In many cases they get important jobs in the administrations of the men they have helped.

Frequently, the only way to document this is by a backward glance at history. Current contributions are clouded by hazy records and by donations that are listed under the names of secretaries, relatives, and friends. Connections between contributions and rewards are not always visible. Only after men close to the event speak out in later years do the items fall into place.

In 1932, William Woodin, formerly a Republican, who had been president of the American Car and Foundry Company, gave early and often to the campaign of Franklin D.

Roosevelt for President. Once he called at campaign headquarters in New York, and a pompous doorman would not admit him to the office of James A. Farley, the campaign manager. Mr Woodin went to a pay telephone and called Mr. Farley to ask how a man with a $50,000 contribution could see the chairman. Mr. Woodin became secretary of the treasury for Mr. Roosevelt.

Among others in that group of contributors for the 1932 campaign were Henry Morgenthau, Sr., and Joseph P. Kennedy. Mr. Morgenthau's son, Henry, Jr., later became secretary of the treasury. Mr. Kennedy became first chairman of the Securities and Exchange Commission and later ambassador to London.

Activists in this and later Roosevelt campaigns were Robert Jackson of New Hampshire, W. Forbes Morgan of New York, and L. W. "Chip" Robert of Georgia. Mr. Jackson developed clients interested in legislation and removed himself from the Democratic National Committee. Mr. Morgan did likewise when various whiskey franchises came to him with the repeal of prohibition. During World War II, Mr. Robert collected too many war contracts to take an active hand in politics. Like Mr. Jackson and Mr. Morgan, he moved off the scene.

Every administration produces illustrations of this kind. Winthrop W. Aldrich, a New York banker, was heavily involved in raising and providing money for General Dwight D. Eisenhower's 1952 campaign. The Republican finance committee headed by Mr. Aldrich was credited with producing $2,250,000 for the campaign. Less than a month after Mr. Eisenhower was elected it was announced that Mr. Aldrich would be the new ambassador to Great Britain. Mr. Aldrich was a man of wide experience and knew his way around the international jungle of finance and diplomacy. This is not always true of diplomatic appointments.

In 1956, the owner of a chain of dress shops gave $26,500 to Republicans. A few months later, he was appointed ambassador to Ceylon. During public hearings by a Senate committee, relating to confirmation by the Senate, he was unable, when

Their money helped elect presidents. William Woodin (lower left), Henry Morganthau, Sr. (upper right), and Joseph P. Kennedy (lower right), who were among the top financial backers of Franklin D. Roosevelt's bid for the presidency in 1932. Winthrop W. Aldrich (upper left), who helped raise the money for General Dwight D. Eisenhower's campaign in 1952.

questioned, to name the prime minister of India or Ceylon.

The influence of fund-raisers in any administration usually is broader than the simple appointment of a few men to jobs. A man with much experience at the White House suggests that the character of a president's administration is set by the people who raise large sums of money for the party. These men always are given a chance to express their views on subjects in which they are interested. They do not always get what they want, but they have a hearing, and they regard this as being of great importance.

Access to the decision maker applies all the way down the line from president to county board of commissioners. The chief collector for one party in a state said his work in producing money had given him a voice in party nominations ranging from mayor to president. He also had a veto power over which demands of his big contributors would be sent to Washington, since they flowed through him.

A hearing at the top, access to the decision maker, a chance to be heard—these things are often more important to big contributors than are contracts.

A striking example of the power of big contributors was provided by the 1952 Democratic Convention in Chicago.

Vice President Alben Barkley went to that convention with many assurances that he had substantial support from President Truman and from the upper levels of organized labor. During a long career in Congress, Mr. Barkley had supported labor causes.

However, half a dozen labor politicians held a meeting and decided that Mr. Barkley, at seventy-four, was too old to be a candidate for president. The labor leaders included Walter Reuther, president of United Automobile Workers, and the directors of labor's political action groups.

Mr. Barkley was shocked when he learned of their decision. He withdrew from the race with a statement saying:

Since arriving in Chicago, I have learned that certain self-appointed labor leaders have taken upon themselves to announce their opposition to me as a Democratic nominee for President. They have admitted to me that weeks ago they committed themselves to a program and to candidates other than myself which would give them greater control of the machinery and policies of the Democratic party.

Another example could be found at the national convention that nominated Mr. Eisenhower for president in 1952, also in Chicago.

In the thick of the battle between followers of Mr. Eisenhower and those of Senator Robert A. Taft of Ohio, a reporter made his way to a small room in a suite in the Sheraton-Blackstone hotel. A man sat at a desk on which was a stack of bills of large denomination. Beside the bills was a note-pad on which were listed the names of important New York financiers with telephone numbers at which they could be reached at any hour of the day.

The job of this man—the political agent for the big money people—was to round up delegate support for Mr. Eisenhower, a small detail that Mr. Eisenhower knew nothing about. Three days later, Mr. Eisenhower was nominated. A few months later, the political agent was serving as a recruiting officer for vital federal posts. Still later, he moved into a position to choose among bidders for large military contracts. Eventually, he went out of the administration under a cloud.

Not long after his defeat, Senator Taft wrote that the greatest factor working against him in the convention was the power of the New York financial interests. He said that these interests and the businessmen subject to their influence had chosen Mr. Eisenhower as their candidate more than a year before the convention.

The business of getting a nomination requires not only money for preconvention campaigning but also support of powerful interests and assurances that money will be provided for the election campaign that is to follow.

Supporters of General Eisenhower, according to Dr. Alexander Heard, calculated in 1951 that it would cost $4 million to get him into the presidential race and win the nomination. The organized work in advance of the convention cost $2.5 million. Time, goods, and services put into work for Mr. Eisenhower by different individuals ran up the price another million or so dollars. And it was estimated that more money was spent in losing the nomination for Senator Taft than in winning it for Mr. Eisenhower.

In 1964, Nelson Rockefeller and William S. Scranton of Pennsylvania were reported to have spent a minimum of $4 million in efforts to win a Republican nomination at San Francisco. Barry Goldwater's backers from the South, the West and the Middle West dumped $5.5 million into their work and took the nomination.

There are no solid estimates of costs in 1968 campaigns. A friend of the late Robert F. Kennedy said when he entered the presidential race that $4 million had been set aside for campaigning in three states. Mr. Kennedy campaigned in four states and wound up more than a million dollars in debt. Hubert Humphrey, who won the nomination without entering a single primary, spent more than a million dollars just to get around the country and talk to the right people. There are no figures on expenditures by Senator Eugene McCarthy of Minnesota and Senator George McGovern of South Dakota. Nor is there a firm estimate of the cost of winning a Republican nomination for Mr. Nixon. One informed Republican suggests $3 million as a good figure—even though Mr. Nixon had no substantial opposition for the nomination.

No law regulates the spending for a presidential nomination. No reports of this spending are required. The identity of individuals or interests supporting a given candidate is regarded as a trade secret, sometimes known only to his fund-raisers. There are laws aimed loosely at controlling the amount of money spent for electing a president after his nomination. The Corrupt Practices Act fixes an upper limit of $3 million for the spending by any committee and a maximum of $5,000 for the gift by any individual to a single committee. Consequently

A typical scene celebrating the nomination of a presidential candidate. This one, of the Republican convention in 1968, marks the end of a decisive stage in Richard M. Nixon's march to the White House. The investment in securing his nomination is estimated at $3 million.

the two major parties set up scores of separate committees, none of which spends as much as $3 million. Everything is technically legal.

In the 1968 presidential race, Republicans spent $29.6 million through forty-six different national committees to elect Richard M. Nixon. Democrats spent $12.6 million through ninety-seven different national groups in trying to elect Hubert Humphrey. George Wallace wrote that he had no committees but that $6.7 million were spent for his campaign.

The total amount, nearly $50 million, covered only the money spent after the nomination of candidates. It included none of the money that went into efforts of different candidates to win presidential nomination, nor any of the money spent by organized labor, by candidates for the Senate and the House of Representatives, and by candidates at state and local levels.

The two major parties will spend at least $180 million in efforts to win control of congressional, state, and local offices in 1970. Combining this with the cost of work by volunteers, the total price for the campaign will rise to about $190 million.

Projected into the 1972 presidential campaign, expenditures may reach $275 million. This money is spread through the whole political spectrum: 15 percent goes for the presidential campaign, 50 percent for statewide campaigns, and 35 percent for congressional and local races. These figures are based on the best evidence available.

In sum, campaign spending is so far out of hand that no one pretends to enforce the regulatory laws. Committees multiply. Reports are filed, and gather dust—and that is the end. Charles Michelson, a great newspaperman in his early days and later a hard-nosed political practitioner, wrote in *The Ghost Talks* in 1944 that the Corrupt Practices Act made "constructive criminals out of all the officials of the two great parties." Each party spends as much as it can raise. Neither asks questions about finances at national, state, or local levels. Not since Senator Thaddeus H. Caraway of Arkansas sifted through campaign spending methods almost forty years ago has there been a full-dress inquiry into the subject.

There are plenty of laws, but none works. The laws are made and enforced by politicians who bend them to fit their needs.

The problem of raising campaign money is a constant worry to politicians. Thoughtful men are troubled by the forces that tug at government; some speak of the danger of an oligarchy. They resent and resist the pressure applied by men and groups that provide campaign money. Still, no one has been able to produce a better way of financing campaigns.

Proposals that a small percentage of tax money be set aside for campaign funds have been rejected. Efforts to make campaign contributions of $25 or $100 deductible items in income taxes have gotten nowhere. Endeavors to raise money by soliciting small amounts from voters do not come close to producing enough to meet the needs of modern campaigning. Although broadcasting companies are given the use of publicly owned air waves, suggestions that candidates be allotted free time on television and radio are waved aside. A few officeholders charge that the Federal Communications Commission is fearful of the broadcasters.

Thus, reliance on big doners continues. Most elective jobs at congressional and state levels cost far more to win than they pay in salaries. And politicians live in constant danger of losing the support either of the men who provide the money or of the voters who cast the ballots.

In this situation, one might conclude that politicians are simply tools of industry or labor. However, other facts of political life come into play to modify such a conclusion:

• Different interests of men who pay for political campaigns bring pressures on officeholders from various directions. Labor wants one thing. Industry wants another. Professional organizations make other demands. Community action groups have their own ideas. All industries do not want the same thing. Out of this mingling of forces comes a compromise that achieves a kind of balance. Politics becomes the art of the possible.

• Quite a few wealthy men in and out of the industrial community give time, thought, and money to politics and want little or nothing from officeholders. They spearhead drives to raise campaign funds for good candidates. Bernard Baruch of New York and South Carolina gave generously of time, advice, and money to politicians of both parties at the presidential and state levels. Robert W. Woodruff of Georgia, whose fortune came from soft drinks, railroads, and banks, worked for stable government in Georgia for years.

• There are times when independent or fusion candidates rise successfully to disrupt the established system, upsetting the major political parties.

Mayor John V. Lindsay of New York, losing the Republican nomination in 1969, ran as an independent and a liberal. He cut deeply into the usual Democratic organization and rallied a section of the Republicans. But Lindsay, like some other successful independents, had the carefully planned support of monied interests, both financial and labor, and the managers of ethnic groups. His campaign had more funds to spend than his opposing camps. The behind-the-scenes powers largely stuck together and just shifted party labels.

While organization and central backing count for much, the powers in the background cannot afford to ignore popular trends and desires, as indicated by the voices of many groups, some small, some growing to formidable size, but not yet represented in the controlling power hierarchy. At times they, too, can disrupt well-established processes, as Eugene McCarthy threatened to do in 1968.

• Often in places of political power there are honest men and women who keep watch over those who soften under pressure. A watchful press corps can provide publicity. And then there is that poll of "customer" opinion which has to be faced at various intervals. When aroused and angry, voters can act.

Thus, while dollars are essential and often dominant in politics, there are other factors which can prove decisive and help serve the public interest.

CHAPTER TWO / **Getting Into Politics**

In view of all the pressures, the hard work, the invasion of privacy, and the uncertainties of politics, why do men and women aspire to public life? Most good politicians could make more money if they invested the same amount of work and time elsewhere. Their answers to the question vary widely.

Governor Nelson Rockefeller of New York, campaigning for a Republican candidate in North Dakota, said: "Many of my friends told me when I was planning to run for office, 'Nelson, politics is a dirty business. Don't let yourself get involved in it.' My reply to them was, 'If politics is a dirty business, it's our fault. It's our business. We should get into politics and clean it up.'"

Mr. Rockefeller was rich enough to pick his own route. He could go in at the top, spend his own money, and make his own decisions. Most officeholders have to take a different approach.

The most common is through community organizations. Men and women work with civic service groups, veterans clubs, and religious and charitable agencies. They get involved with business, professional, labor, and farm organizations. Here they move into a position of leadership and develop a following.

Next thing they know, the bug has bitten them. They are in politics. Senator Abraham Ribicoff of Connecticut put it this way:

> Most candidates run to have a say in public affairs. Whether the issue is city traffic, state funds for education, or peace in the world, candidates go one step further than the average citizen. They not only have opinions on what should be done, they want the chance to put those opinions to work.[1]

Many persons choose politics as the road to publicity and power. They want the feel of being close to the mighty, perhaps of being a part of history. They have an urge to be in the middle of important happenings. They want to get on television, to see their name in the newspaper. Others calculate that publicity flowing from the simple act of running for office will bring more customers into their business, more clients into their law office.

However, the greatest number of people probably are drawn into public life because they enjoy this activity. They like people, and they wish to serve. The work is hard. The hours are long. They are always on display. Constituents are demanding. Often they have to compromise on issues they regard as important. Yet they remain in the field.

Some are drawn into politics by a moment of challenge or inspiration.

John Nance Garner, as a young lawyer in Uvalde, Texas, went to a state political convention. Years later, he told a friend: "I saw all those big people there. I looked them over and said to myself, 'I'm just as good as they are. I can do just as well.'" In 1902, Mr. Garner was elected to the House of Representatives. He climbed through the Ways and Means Committee to the speakership and finally to the vice presidency. He spent 38 years in Washington.

[1] Ribicoff, Abraham, and Newman, Jon O. *Politics: The American Way.* Boston: Allyn and Bacon, 1967. p. 39.

Sam Rayburn, Speaker of the House longer than any man in history, said:

> I was just 12 years old when Joseph W. Bailey, then a Congressman from Texas, came to Bonham to speak. Our farm was several miles from Bonham. I walked through the rain to hear him. I was a timid country boy. When I got there, the town folks had crowded in and gotten all the seats. I stood for two hours and listened while the rain dripped down the back of my neck from the edge of the roof. I was so carried away with what I heard that I vowed that one day I would be Speaker of the House.

As a young man, Gale McGee heard a speech by the then Senator George W. Norris of Nebraska. Mr. McGee went on to become a teacher, broadcaster, writer, and legislative aide to a senator from Wyoming—and at the age of 43 made it to the Senate from that state.

The general mix of men who find their way into politics is about the average of the community from which they come, except that most have more schooling. Candidates for public office usually are high school graduates. In the upper reaches, almost all members of Congress and governors are college graduates.

Among professions, lawyers head the list. This applies to all levels of politics. One reason is that the lawyer knows where to find campaign money. He is accustomed to talking on his feet. His work compels him to be something of an actor. It teaches him the twists and turns through the social and political structure of his community. Having been trained in law, the rules of politics come easy.

Congress provides a fair sample of the kind of people in politics across the nation. A majority of congressmen come from some layer of local politics. Sixty-seven percent of the Senate and 53 percent of the House members are lawyers. This is an average of 60 percent, which is about the same proportion found in state legislatures. Their predominance inspired the thought that lawyers make the laws for other lawyers to interpret for paying clients.

In numbers, businessmen rank next to lawyers among politicians. They come from all kinds of business.

The late Everett McKinley Dirksen of Illinois once ran a dredging company, then a wholesale bakery. John J. Williams of Delaware is a feed and grain merchant. Paul J. Fannin of Arizona deals in oil and farm chemicals. Wallace F. Bennett of Utah has an automobile agency as well as interests in paint and glass companies. Winston Prouty of Vermont runs a lumber company and has banking interests. These are a few samples from the United States Senate. Banking and investment people are found at many levels of politics.

Teachers, writers, and radio and television people also tend to gravitate into politics. They are trained to express their ideas in something less than four-syllable words. They develop the knack of selling themselves and their ideas, and are found sprinkled through state legislatures, the upper levels of state government, and both houses of Congress.

Of the senators, Karl E. Mundt of South Dakota was a high school and college teacher before he turned to farming, real estate, and politics. Eugene J. McCarthy of Minnesota taught social science, economics, and sociology in high schools and colleges. John T. Tower of Texas taught political science in a small college until he joined seventy other Texans in the scramble for the Senate seat vacated by Lyndon Johnson when he became vice president. Mr. Johnson himself had once been a teacher. Mark Hatfield of Oregon was a political science teacher before he became a member of the state legislature, then governor, and finally senator.

Among those from the field of communications, Governor Jack Williams of Arizona, Governor Tom McCall of Oregon, and Representative H. R. Gross of Iowa, were broadcasters. Representative Edith Green of Oregon was a radio announcer and script writer, as well as a teacher. The late Joseph Martin, a former Speaker of the House, was a newspaper reporter when he turned to politics.

Different Paths to Politics

Richard C. Lee, for many years mayor of New Haven, Connecticut, was a news reporter of city hall when he decided he would rather be a politician than write about them. Others who stepped from journalism into the House of Representatives included F. Edward Hebert of Louisiana, a copy boy and sports reporter; and Roman C. Pucinski of Illinois, Daniel E. Button of New York, and Tom Steed of Oklahoma, working newsmen. Clarence J. Brown of Ohio is one of several publishers in the House.

Different incidents and issues combine to bring men into the limelight and set them on the road to politics.

Lester Maddox, governor of Georgia, ran a restaurant in Atlanta. He closed it rather than serve Negroes and rode the segregation issue into office. George Wallace of Alabama tried to use the same issue to lift himself into the presidency.

Claude R. Kirk of Florida developed an insurance and investment business. In 1964 he backed Barry Goldwater, caught the public fancy, and was elected governor. Ronald Reagan, an actor, also figured prominently in the Goldwater campaign. He won the support of influential Californians and they helped to land him in the governor's mansion.

All of these men followed one of the first rules of politics: they caught a wave of publicity which made their names known to the public. This is done in many ways at both the community and the national level.

James A. Farley started as a first baseman for a baseball team at Grassy Point, New York, took advantage of his local publicity to win election as town clerk, and wound up as chairman of the Democratic National Committee and postmaster general.

Charles E. Goodell of New York, now in the Senate, was one of the best catchers on the Williams College baseball team. For a time, he played semiprofessional baseball. He moved through a variety of civic, church, and party activities to the House of Representatives before being appointed to the Senate.

Robert B. Mathias of California won the Decathlon events

in two sets of Olympic games before going to the House of Representatives. Among his athletic companions in that branch of Congress are Gerald Ford of Michigan and Wilmer D. Mizell of North Carolina. Mr. Ford played football so well at the University of Michigan that he was offered jobs with the Green Bay Packers and the Detroit Lions. Instead, he chose politics. Mr. Mizell went further into professional athletics. He pitched for the St. Louis Cardinals and represented the National League in the 1959 All-Star game before joining the House.

A wide variety of other opportunities has served as a springboard into politics.

John E. Fogarty, a House member from Rhode Island, was a bricklayer. At twenty-three, he was elected president of Bricklayers Union No. 1 in his state, served four terms, then came to Congress.

George P. Miller of California was running a travel agency when the great depression dried up his business. Once, things got so bad that he worked as a street sweeper to qualify for relief. Later, he got a job with Veterans Bureau, then moved through American Legion work to the state legislature and on to Congress.

The route taken by Harold E. Hughes of Iowa is unique. He grew up on a farm in a deeply religious family. World War II interfered with his studies at the University of Iowa. He became a rifleman and a private and saw fourteen months of combat in Tunisia, Sicily, and Italy. At the end of the war, he emerged from the Army so shaken by the fighting that he turned to hard drinking.

After several years of this, Mr. Hughes joined Alcoholics Anonymous and the Methodist church. He thought of becoming a minister. Instead, he became a truck driver and developed his own trucking line. This work led him into becoming a field agent for the Iowa Motor Trucking Association, traveling over the state to sell memberships. Dissatisfied with the kind of help the association was giving small truckers, Mr. Hughes set up his own agency. As business flourished, he developed an insurance agency and a real estate abstract office.

Mr. Hughes entered politics by accident. He took a complaint to the state commerce commission, got no satisfaction, and went to the governor's office to speak his mind. The governor suggested that he run for election to the commission. Mr. Hughes did, and he won. Four years later, he became governor. He served three terms before moving to the United States Senate.

In the period since 1941, hundreds of combat veterans from three wars have found their way into politics. Dozens of them are spread through the upper levels of government.

Governor Raymond P. Shafer of Pennsylvania was a small-town lawyer at the beginning of World War II. In the war, he commanded a PT boat in the South Pacific which completed eighty missions, and was awarded a medal for taking seventeen paratroopers off Corregidor in a rubber dinghy under sniper fire. John H. Chafee, former governor of Rhode Island and later secretary of the navy for Mr. Nixon, went ashore with the First Marine division in the initial landing at Guadalcanal. He fought again with a front-line rifle company in Korea.

Among senators, Philip A. Hart of Michigan was wounded in the D-Day invasion of Normandy and emerged with five or six decorations. Howard Cannon of Nevada was overseas for twenty months with the Air Force, was shot down behind enemy lines in Holland, and dodged Germans for forty-two days before getting back to American troops. He flew in the lead airplane in the invasion of France and later joined the French underground movement. He came home with too many decorations to count.

In the House, Craig Hosmer of California commanded navy gun crews on merchant tankers running the German blockade in the North Atlantic, then shifted to the Pacific for the battles of Iwo Jima and Okinawa, and finally was in the group that landed General Douglas MacArthur at Tokyo and put occupation troops ashore at Hiroshima. John A. Blatnik of Minnesota was a paratrooper with the Army Air Force Intelligence and the Office of Strategic Services. Speaking the native language, he spent eight months behind enemy lines in Yugoslavia, working with partisans, gathering information about the enemy, and helping rescue American airmen.

Few men can match the records of Senator Daniel K. Inouye and Representative Spark Matsunaga of Hawaii, both of whom served in the famous 442nd Regiment Combat Team, a unit composed entirely of Nisei volunteers.

Mr. Inouye was born in Honolulu. His father was a department store clerk. He went into World War II as a private. While leading a platoon in destroying three machine gun nests in the Po valley, Mr. Inouye was shot in the stomach and legs. His arm was shattered by a grenade. He continued to direct the assualt before allowing himself to be evacuated. He lost an arm in the fighting and came out of the war as a captain.

Mr. Matsunaga was an original member of the same unit, going in as a second lieutenant. He served with it in North Africa and Europe, was twice wounded, and also wound up as a captain. The unit itself has been called the most decorated in history.

Both men drifted into politics through the practice of law, entered the public prosecutor's office in Honolulu, made the Territorial legislature and, finally, reached Congress.

Like most people who make a success in politics, they had a reputation of accomplishment in their own communities on which to build. The war had given them a running start. They were known to the voters—and to friends who would help to finance campaigns.

For most politicians, the progress is slower and less dramatic. They move into office at the city or county level and gradually move upward. Here are a few random samples:

George D. Aiken grew up on his father's farm in Vermont. As a youngster, he had a patch of raspberries. Through the years, he turned this into a 500-acre nursery and became a pioneer in the cultivation of wild flowers. He helped develop a county farm cooperative and served for seventeen years as school director for his home town. He was elected to the state House of Representatives and wound up as Speaker of that branch of the legislature. From this point, his course took him to lieutenant governor and governor. He had held almost every elective office in the state before he became United States senator.

James A. Rhodes dropped out of Ohio State University during the depression to help his family. He developed the ambition to be mayor of his home city of Columbus. The first step was as ward committeeman for his party. Next, he was a member of the school board. After that, he became city auditor and then mayor. Three terms in that office helped to boost him to state auditor, where he stayed for ten years. In 1962, he became governor of Ohio, serving two four-year terms.

Richard J. Daley traveled all through the lower levels of his party before he came into power in Chicago. Born near the stockyards, he sold newspapers as a youngster, then worked in the stockyards by day and went to DePaul University at night. With a law degree and friendly ties to the Democratic machine, he spent the next two years in the state legislature. In 1946, he ran for sheriff of Cook County and was beaten. The party bosses found a place for him as deputy comptroller of Cook County.

Three years later, Governor Adlai Stevenson, in a bow to the powerful Chicago organization, appointed Mr. Daley director of the state department of finance. Mr. Daley was hard-working and had his eyes on the future. He moved into the inner circles of Mr. Stevenson's organization and served as a consultant on legislation. A year later, he went home to Chicago and was elected Cook County clerk. After four years in this job, he became mayor and eased into the chairmanship of the Cook County Democratic Committee, securing control of the most powerful big-city machine in the nation, with a voice in choosing presidents.

Wright Patman of Texas is one of the few men left in public life who actually was born in a log cabin. It consisted of three rooms and stood on his parents' cotton farm in the northeast corner of Texas. He rode a mule six miles to school, lit the fires in the morning, swept the building at night, studied law by

Different Paths to Politics

VIA PRESS

Thomas McCall
Governor, Oregon

Edith Green
Representative, Ore.

H. R. Gross
Representative, Iowa

Joseph Martin
Ex-Speaker of House

VIA SPORTS

James A. Farley
Ex-Postmaster General

Charles E. Goodell
Senator, New York

Robert B. Mathias
Representative, Calif.

Gerald R. Ford
Representative, Mich.

VIA HEROISM

John H. Chafee
Secretary of Navy

Craig Hosmer
Representative, Calif.

Daniel K. Inoye
Senator, Hawaii

John A. Blatnik
Representative, Minn.

himself, and raised cotton to pay for his last year in college. A storm destroyed the cotton. Patman and another student lived that year on campus in a house so rickety that they took turns staying awake to meet the possibility that the roof might fall in.

He began in politics as assistant to the prosecuting attorney in his home county. Next came two terms in the state legislature, then five years as district attorney. He put his career on the line in a fight against the Ku Klux Klan, built a reputation across his congressional district, and reached the House of Representatives in 1928. By the rules of seniority, forty years later he became chairman of the powerful Banking and Currency Committee.

Personal wealth can ease the road of a man aspiring to a political career. Often it enables him to skip some of the tough chores at the lower levels. The careers of Averell Harriman, Franklin D. Roosevelt, and the Kennedy brothers illustrate this point.

John F. Kennedy moved directly into the House of Representatives and climbed quickly through the Senate to the presidency. Robert F. Kennedy stepped into a post with a congressional committee, ran a campaign for his brother John, leaped into a Senate seat, and was gambling for the presidency when he was assassinated. The youngest brother, Edward, reached the Senate in his first try.

Franklin Roosevelt was drawn into politics in his county by party leaders who thought he would come across with campaign money to help the Democrats in a region that was held almost solidly by Republicans. He won, and was on his way. Later, an argument used in the inner councils of the Democrats for his nomination as governor of New York was that he could finance his own campaign if necessary.

The environment of wealth often has more influence on the politicians making these choices than does the personal fortune of the candidate himself. The calculation is that the wealthy candidate has rich friends who will pool their resources in support of his campaign. This does not always work.

Averell Harriman, a substantial contributor to the presidential campaigns of Franklin Roosevelt, served in the Roosevelt cabinet in various important posts. Later, he became governor of New York. He was beaten for reelection by another millionaire, Nelson Rockefeller. In one of Mr. Harriman's campaigns for governor, a wealthy friend was asked to contribute. The man said: "I've got three million dollars. Harriman's got forty. Let him use his own money."

Forty million dollars was underrating Mr. Harriman. He is no poor man, even by Rockefeller standards. Mr. Harriman had a head start of $100 million left by his father, E. H. Harriman, who was called the nation's outstanding railroad man when he died in 1909. The Union Pacific was only one of the railroads he controlled.

During college years, Averell spent his summer vacations working in the offices and shops of the Union Pacific. After college, he worked with a railroad inspection gang, then was a surveyor, a locomotive fireman, and a laborer in railroad shops. When he came into his own, he headed the Union Pacific and Illinois Central railroads, then turned to investments, a trust company, and banking.

A point of pride with Mr. Harriman was his achievement in improving relations between management and the workers of the Union Pacific. In the 1932 presidential campaign, Mr. Roosevelt called on him for advice about railroad policy and Mr. Harriman stepped naturally into various other duties.

Prescott Bush of Connecticut felt the Harriman touch. Mr. Bush was born in Ohio and educated at Yale. He was a captain in the bloody Meuse-Argonne offensive in World War I. After the war, his path led him through hardware and rubber companies into the Harriman banking concern, then into a private banking company and various corporations. On the side, Mr. Bush had a solid interest in social welfare and civic problems that eventually took him to the United States Senate.

Personal friendship brought John V. Lindsay of New York City into politics. His father was an investment banker. He was born on Riverside Drive and educated at Yale and Yale

Law School. In college, he met Herbert Brownell, a Wall Street lawyer who managed the drives that won presidential nominations for Thomas E. Dewey and General Eisenhower. Mr. Brownell eased the way for Mr. Lindsay into a law firm.

In 1952, Mr. Brownell took Mr. Lindsay to the Republican National Convention to help in the fight for Mr. Eisenhower's nomination. Later, as attorney general for Mr. Eisenhower, Mr. Brownell took Mr. Lindsay to Washington to work as his assistant. Mr. Lindsay moved on to the House of Representatives and later became mayor of New York City.

And many lesser fortunes are to be found sprinkled through various levels of government.

Behind J. William Fulbright of Arkansas stood an Oxford education and a family fortune in lumber, banks, farms, real estate, a newspaper, and other enterprises. Mr. Fulbright moved first into the House of Representatives, then to the Senate. Senator Barry Goldwater of Arizona was a department store heir. The two Morton Brothers—Thruston, a former senator from Kentucky, and Rogers C. B., a House member from Maryland and chairman of the Republican National Committee—were supported in their ambitions by great wealth derived from flour mills and banks.

Many other men made their fortunes in business or in a profession before seeking elective office.

Charles A. Percy of Illinois worked his way up the ladder with a photographic supply firm before he became a U. S. senator. Stuart Symington built his fortune from an electrical manufacturing company; he was drawn into government by President Truman and later became a senator from Missouri. Everett Jordan of North Carolina created a rich textile business before he became a senator.

Jacob Javits grew up in a New York City ghetto. His father was a janitor. Mr. Javits made his first million as a lawyer specializing in bankruptcy cases. In 1946, he was elected to the House of Representatives from New York City in a district that Republicans thought could not be won. He held the district for ten years before transferring to the Senate.

Different Paths to Politics

VIA WEALTH	VIA ENTERPRISE	VIA FAMILY

Franklin D. Roosevelt
32nd President

Charles H. Percy
Senator, Illinois

Adlai E. Stevenson III
Illinois

John F. Kennedy
35th President

Jacob K. Javits
Senator, New York

Bronson LaFollette
Wisconsin

Averell Harriman
Ex-Governor, New York

Walter J. Hickel
Secretary of Interior

Henry Cabot Lodge
Massachusetts

Nelson A. Rockefeller
Governor, New York

Hiram L. Fong
Senator, Hawaii

James Symington
Representative, Mo.

Walter J. Hickel was the eldest of a Kansas tenant farmer's ten children. He went to Alaska when he was twenty, arriving with thirty-seven cents in his pocket, earned a modest stake, and plunged into the wartime building boom. As the money piled up, Mr. Hickel invested in hotels and shopping centers and entered politics as a millionaire. He served as governor of Alaska before becoming secretary of the interior.

Perhaps the greatest Horatio Alger story of them all is that of Hiram Leong Fong, senator from Hawaii. He grew up at the far end of the field with three downs against him. His father and mother came to Hawaii from the Kwangtung province of China as indentured laborers on a sugar plantation. His father earned $12 a month. Hiram was the seventh of eleven children. The family lived in a tough slum district of Honolulu.

Young Hiram shined shoes, sold newspapers, and worked his way through high school. He worked three years to save money to go to the University of Hawaii—as a clerk, collecting bills, guiding tourists. At the university, he still found time to edit the newspaper, debate, and make the volleyball and rifle teams. Two more years of work were spent earning money to go to Harvard Law School.

Mr. Fong got back to Hawaii with a law degree and a dime. He worked as a municipal clerk, then as deputy city attorney in Honolulu. He founded the first interracial law firm in the islands: Fong, Miho, Choy, and Robinson—Chinese, Japanese, Korean, and Caucasian. Mr. Fong put his money into real estate, insurance, shopping centers, finance, and a banana plantation. He is president of half a dozen firms and his fortune runs into the millions. He served fourteen years in the Territorial legislature and stepped easily into the United States Senate when his state was admitted to the Union.

Personal wealth, however, is not enough to keep a man in office unless he has a talent for getting along with people.

Senator Thruston Morton would stop at a pay station to return a telephone call to a person whom he knew only casually. Mayor John Lindsay prowled through the streets of Negro areas in New York City during racial disturbances of 1968, often without an escort, talking with whomever he met.

Winthrop Rockefeller as a young man worked on construction gangs and met rough and tumble men on their own level, long before he thought of being governor of Arkansas. Governor Nelson Rockefeller once leaped off a speaker's platform in North Dakota and trotted a hundred yards down the side of a hill to shake hands with a group of Indians who were putting on a tribal dance. Franklin Roosevelt once spent an hour in the midst of a campaign showing ship models to a youngster of seven.

Many men turn naturally to politics as a part of family tradition. A place is ready for them. They inherit a ready-made group of supporters and a name that everyone knows.

The fourth generation of Stevensons is busy in Illinois. Adlai Stevenson III is state treasurer. His father was governor, twice a presidential nominee, and ambassador to the United Nations. Lewis G. Stevenson, his grandfather, was secretary of state and chairman of the Board of Pardons in Illinois; he also managed gold and copper mines in Arizona and New Mexico for Mrs. Phoebe Hearst and at one time ran forty-nine farms with a total of 10,500 acres in Illinois, Indiana, and Iowa. The original Adlai Stevenson, great-grandfather of the present bearer of the name, was vice president for Grover Cleveland and sometimes called the "Headsman" by his enemies because he was credited with removing 40,000 Republican postmasters from office.

In Wisconsin, young Bronson LaFollette met his first defeat in 1968 in a race for governor. Three generations of his family have been in politics. His father, Robert M. LaFollette, Jr., was U. S. senator. His uncle Phillip was governor. His grandfather, the original Robert M. LaFollette, dominated Wisconsin politics for a generation as governor and senator and created his own "Progressive" party to run for president.

In Massachusetts, Henry Cabot Lodge comes from a family that has been in politics from the very beginning. George Cabot was a delegate to the state convention that ratified the Constitution of the United States. He served in the United

States Senate from 1791 to 1796, then was secretary of the navy for John Adams. His great-grandson was the original Henry Cabot Lodge who six times was elected to the Senate from Massachusetts. George Lodge, son and secretary of Henry Cabot Lodge, was the father of another Henry Cabot Lodge who was beaten by John F. Kennedy in a race for reelection and who later served three presidents in diplomatic posts.

Representative James Symington of Missouri is a son of Senator Stuart Symington of the same state. His grandfather was James M. Wadsworth, a senator and House member from New York. And still another branch on the family tree was John Hay, secretary of state for William McKinley and Theodore Roosevelt.

Representative James Kee of West Virginia is the third member of his family to hold the same office; both his father and his mother held it before him. Hubert Humphrey's father was an alderman, a mayor, and a member of the state legislature. The great-grandfather of Gaylord Nelson, senator from Wisconsin, helped to organize the Republican party in his state. Senator Nelson is a Democrat.

Whatever the personal circumstances and the particular path to office, the aspiring politician has virtually no prospect of success unless he can draw upon a central source of power —the political party—examined in a later chapter.

CHAPTER THREE / **Pressure on Politicians**

Government in the United States has become the biggest business in the world. Federal, state, and local government agencies are spending at the rate of $300 billion a year. One volume that lists only federal government programs is 670 pages long. A printed copy of the federal budget is about the size of the telephone directory for a large city.

Money is not all that is at stake. Government affects every aspect of American life. It sets the rules of behavior for individuals, corporations, and labor unions.

Personal standards and social behavior are defined for individuals. Laws reach into the neighborhood, the schools, the places where people work. They affect radio, television, the fine arts, marriage, sex, drinking, gambling, the whole area of leisure. Public concern over our natural environment is taking government into efforts to check pollution of air and water. Thus everyone is affected by the acts of the politician—and the politician is subject to strong pressures in the background.

These pressures are no less powerful at the local and state levels than at the federal level. In counties and cities, interested parties press politicians for zoning permits, licenses, a road or street across their property, or a contract to sell supplies. Sometimes the heat gets so intense in a conflict between what these men want and what the public wants that county or local politicians pass a problem along to state officials rather than deal with it themselves, out in the open where voters can see what is happening.

At the state level, pressures are even stronger. States levy taxes, run elections, set up court procedures, and administer civil and criminal law. They authorize and regulate banking, charter corporations, and enjoy wide powers in the fields of health standards, safety, and morals. They operate and support public schools, colleges, and special educational programs. They run prisons and parole and probation boards. They build highways and hospitals, set the ground rules for local government, and regulate the rates of many public service corporations. At every step along the way, there is some man or group of men who would like to have a special favor.

If each state and local community could handle its own affairs, things would be much simpler. State, county, and city lines are invisible. People travel in and out of cities and states to work. Goods move across boundary lines. So do crime, foul air, and dirty water; 100 million automobiles, buses, and trucks; and thousands of trains and airplanes. Such matters require an overall umpire with more authority than a single state. The federal government serves as that umpire.

After 180 years, the role of the umpire has grown enormously. Two world wars and a great depression brought a multiplicity of agencies. They regulate all sorts of things. And once created, they are extremely hard to get rid of. The National Screw Thread Commission is one example. It came into being in 1918 to standardize the width between threads on screws and still was working away happily 16 years later when its functions were turned over to another agency.

New concerns with air, water, education, and the poor are multiplying the number of government agencies. Just before the Nixon administration was installed, a Senate committee found 172 aid programs sprinkled through different departments of government. The Eighty-ninth Congress set up 17 new resource programs, 21 to deal with health, 15 for economic development, 17 for education, 12 to deal with city problems, and 4 for manpower training. The Office of Education had 112 different programs operating under 26 separate grants of power from Congress.

Agencies often overlap and tackle the same problems from different points of view. There is little cooperation among them. Each builds its own power structure, grinds its own axe until the axe becomes more important than the tree it is supposed to cut down. Former Governor Terry Sanford of North Carolina found that in one medium-sized southern city a single family had been helped during the space of two years by sixteen different governmental and private agencies. Each agency had its own rules, interests, and standards. Each tackled the problem differently.

The effort of the federal government to set standards for states through grants-in-aid sometimes goes to ridiculous extremes. An example was a dispute between the Bureau of Public Roads and the Wyoming Highway Department over the color of paint used to mark the outer edge of roads in that state. Wyoming used yellow. The Bureau of Public Roads said it, like the rest of the country, must use white. The Wyoming Highway Department had to yield, but an official said: "Let them come out here and find one of their white lines during one of our blizzards." The Wyoming people had found that a yellow line could be seen on a wintry day. A white line simply vanished in the snow.

The color of paint is not of prime interest to the back-room managers. They can develop a high temperature, however, over the selection of a key man in a federal agency. These are the people who decide where a road is to be built, what regulations are to be laid down for handling drugs, where a military or naval base is to be located, which parts of air or space programs are to be cancelled, or how much rent stockmen shall pay for grazing lands in the West.

In the 1950s the Interior Department set up district advisory boards of western cattlemen to secure their cooperation in handling federal grazing lands. The cattlemen established state groups and a national council to advise the director of the grazing service how much to charge for letting livestock eat the grass on public land. As long as the director listened to their recommendations, all went well.

Then the secretary of the interior appointed a new director who felt that higher fees should be charged. The man whom the council of stockmen had recommended was rejected. The National Council enlisted the help of a powerful senator from a western state. A House appropriations subcommittee got into the hassle. Before the incident was over, the budget of the grazing service was cut 50 percent and the new director was relieved of his duties.

The incident illustrates the value to an interest group of having a friendly hand at the controls of a government agency. This gives the man, or men, behind the scenes access to the person who is making decisions that affect their interests. When the power groups are not permitted to pick the key man in an agency dealing with their affairs, they often obtain a veto over the person selected. Now and then, they manage to do this by writing the qualifications of the man to be selected. Quite often, however, their power is direct and persuasive.

Instances appear in every presidential administration. Under Mr. Eisenhower, the American Farm Bureau Federation and its allies got important posts in the Agriculture Department. When President Kennedy came in, these appointees were replaced by spokesmen for the Farmers Union, which had been a close ally of the Democrats.

In the Kennedy administration, the AFL-CIO, as key spokesman for labor unions, placed one of its important leaders in the post of secretary of labor, another union man as undersecretary, and a prominent union lobbyist as assistant secretary. A union official went into an important decision making job in the housing and home finance agency in whose operations labor had a direct interest.

In a farewell address to the nation on January 17, 1961, President Eisenhower said:

The conjunction of an enormous military establishment and a large arms industry is new in American experience. The total influence—economic, political, even spiritual—is felt in every city, every statehouse, every office of the federal government. We recognize the imperative need for this development. Yet we need not fail to comprehend its grave implications. Our toil, resources and livelihood are all involved; so is the very structure of our society.

In the councils of government, we must guard against the acquisition of unwarranted influence, whether sought or unsought, by the military-industrial complex. The potential for the disastrous rise of misplaced power exists and will persist.

We must never let the weight of this combination endanger our liberties or democratic processes. We should take nothing for granted. Only an alert and knowledgeable citizenry can compel the proper meshing of the huge industrial and military machine of defense with our peaceful methods and goals so that security and liberty may prosper together.

A little later that same year, Speaker Sam Rayburn told a friend:

I have never allowed a defense plant or military base to be established in my Congressional district. I know the time will come when these things must be closed and I do not want my friends in this district put out of work. It is better for the community to grow naturally than to have it developed by pumping Federal money into it.

Various cases point up the significance of the views of these two men. In 1969, for example, opposition arose in Congress to a $5.3 billion contract with an aviation concern for development and production of huge cargo planes for the armed forces. Senator William Proxmire of Wisconsin said that the company had underestimated by $2 billion the cost of the planes and that the total original appropriation had been used up in preliminary work. Under pressure from the Pentagon and industry, the Senate refused to halt the work.

Prior to this decision, industrialists were busy turning the heat on the senators. The prime contractor for building the planes had thousands of subcontractors around the nation. One senator said he had been told by bankers and businessmen in his state that trimming funds for the planes would bring unemployment and might spark a recession.

An example of massive pressure by an industry is that applied at both the federal and the state levels by oil producers, refiners, and distributors. They have had a skilled and highly-paid group of experts busy in Washington for more than a century, beginning in 1866 when a federal tax was levied on crude oil. Pennsylvania producers brought pressure on Congress and the tax was repealed. Since then, the oil industry has been watchful.

In a strictly literal sense, most of the men who work for the industry in Washington and at state legislatures are not lobbyists. They are lawyers, former government and congressional people, public relations consultants, former newsmen who serve as advisors and agents, trade association representatives, sales officers, company vice presidents in charge of governmental relations, or company legal counsels. Far down the line, a few men of lesser status call themselves lobbyists. Across the country, there are "grassroots" spokesmen who spread the good word about oil companies and funnel money into political campaigns.

The stake is a big one. More than a fourth of the land area in the United States is under lease for oil and gas exploration. More than 10 million persons are employed by the oil industry. Oil powers engines for automobiles, ships, railroads, and airplanes, and a variety of motors down to lawn mowers and water pumps. As far back as 1958, when the United States was largely at peace, the military was spending more than a billion dollars a year for 260 million barrels of jet fuel, aviation gasoline, and other petroleum products. It has been estimated that more than 2 million gallons of oil would be required to drive an atomic-powered submarine like the Nautilus the 62,500 miles that it went before changing its nuclear core.

Selling oil to government is only one aspect of the industry's interest. In one form or another, oil goes into chemicals, paints, detergents, insecticides, medicines, fertilizers, synthetic rubber and fibers, asphalt, heating, lubrication, and other goods and processes. Every action of government in widely differing fields is kept under observation.

One oil company set up a political action program with an office in Washington. Its experts are assigned to legislative, foreign, public relations, and tax matters. Another oil company has a staff that varies in size according to need. A third has company executives who work with trade associations on land leases.

Lawyers specialize in keeping track of the leases by oil companies of public lands from the Interior Department. In this group, there were at one time the former chief counsels of the Geological Survey and of the Bureau of Land Management. One lawyer who represented different oil companies on a fee basis became such an authority on federal leasing that he helped Senate and House committees write bills and committee reports dealing with mineral leases.

When tough problems arise, oil companies pool their resources to influence the outcome of legislation affecting their industry. One example is the long struggle to keep intact the oil depletion allowance of 27½ percent.

This came into effect in 1913 after the income tax was adopted. It permitted persons with income from mining and similar industries to deduct up to 5 percent of their gross income in figuring taxes. During World War I, these allowances were raised for oil producers to induce them to explore and drill. It was feared that oil discoveries would not keep pace with needs. By 1926, the depletion allowances for oil had been raised to 27½ percent, now being trimmed to 22 percent. Only half of net income could be treated in this manner.

Because of these allowances, it was charged that oil companies did not feel the full impact of excess profits taxes as did other industries in World War II. One senator figured that in a ten-year period, twenty-seven major oil companies had a total income before taxes of more than $3 billion. They paid corporate taxes to the federal government of $562 million, at a rate that was calculated at 17 percent. In the same period, other enterprises were paying at a rate of 52 percent.

The fight to keep the depletion allowance at a high level continued for years and brought into action all of the pressure resources of the companies at every critical stage of the game. No one could guess how much money had gone into this work.

In 1969, oil men were busy campaigning against any revision of the tax laws that would increase the levies on the industry. Some of them said such taxes would be paid by consumers through higher prices on gasoline and fuel oil. One spokesman for the oil industry said privately that a different method might be used. "I know one way we can recoup our losses," he said. "We can save a lot on campaign contributions."

A small hint of the cost of a full-scale drive by the oil industry for legislation emerged in 1956 and again in 1958. At that time, the oil and gas industry was trying to pass a law which would strip the Federal Power Commission of authority to regulate prices charged by producers of natural gas sold in interstate commerce. The Supreme Court had ruled that the commission had such power.

The gas and oil industry mounted a massive effort to get a measure through Congress that would have the effect of overruling the Supreme Court. Special committees were organized to direct the campaign. A public relations firm got $100,000 for shaping plans for the drive. A poll of business and professional leaders was taken; it suggested that the public was opposed to the measure sought by the oil and gas companies. A campaign was undertaken to change public opinion. All of the mass media were used. Advertisements were placed in more than a thousand newspapers. There were interviews, articles, and hundreds of radio and television broadcasts. A special film was made. Information kits went to farmers and businessmen. Leaflets were tucked into customer bills. Speeches were made to civic organizations. One estimate said that more than $2 million went into the campaign between 1954 and 1956, not counting the expenses of individual corporations or the 3,000 oil and gas company employees used.

Hard work pushed the bill through the House of Representatives. Passage by the Senate seemed certain. Suddenly all of the work and money was made useless by the misstep of one oil company. It hired a lobbyist who was unwise enough to make campaign contributions to several senators who favored passage of the bill. One senator repudiated the contribution and charged that it represented a bribe. He told the Senate he would change his vote and oppose the bill. The measure squeaked through the Senate and died at the hands of President Eisenhower.

The president, who favored the principles of the bill, vetoed it because of what he called "arrogant lobbying." A single campaign contribution of $2,500, made by a lobbyist to the wrong man, killed the bill.

Instances of outright bribery among elected officials in Washington rarely come to the surface. Lobbyists and members of Congress alike regard this method of obtaining action from the federal government as not effective. "Direct bribery simply is not a significant element in the influence pattern at Washington," said one lobbyist. Congressmen and their legislative staffs agree with this appraisal. A watchful press corps and an opposition party always are eager to bring such attempts into the open.

Congressmen who served in legislatures of different states before going to Washington report that bribery, lobbying, and influence peddling are more prevalent and open to observation in state capitols than in Congress. Here are a few cases:

The *Texas Observer*, edited for years by Ronnie Dugger at the edge of the campus of the University of Texas, printed a list of items provided for members of the state legislature.

These included food, trips to Mexico and to Kentucky race-tracks, hunting trips aboard an oil-company yacht, plus tips on oil stock and oil leases. Principal donors were listed as oil, gas, and construction companies interested usually in tax rates, oil leases, royalty payments on oil lands, and contracts from the state.

In Florida, lobbyists are required to file reports of their spending. During the first month of the 1969 legislative session, the Homebuilders Association gave a $5,000 party for lawmakers. Racetrack agents spent $900 and got a bill to allow summer racing. The beer industry spent $600 to keep good will. The Florida Phosphate Council came up with $434 for meals and entertainment; a bill to levy a severance tax on the industry was killed.

In Georgia, a legislator was critical of the number of members of the legislature who were on retainers from one or another industry. "This is buying influence," he said. "It's a legal pay-off. You can bet that if they are on a retainer with some company interested in a bill they are not going to vote against the company's point of view. We ought to pass a law to require all legislators to disclose who has them on retainers."

In the states, members of the legislature are more easily reached and often more vulnerable than are members of Congress. Few state legislators have any place to work except in their hotel rooms. Pay and expense allowances often are inadequate. In many states, lobbyists set up their offices in hotels where they live and work in the midst of the legislators. They pick up meal checks for members of the legislature and provide transportation for them, along with drinks and a wide variety of entertainment. A study of the California legislature suggested that this worked out well for the lobbyists.

It was in California that Artie Samish established such a hold over the legislature in the late 1940s that he came to be called the "secret boss" of the state. He built something approaching a political machine of his own by providing campaign funds and living expenses for legislators. The liquor, racetrack, and business interests that he represented cared little about general legislation. What they chiefly wanted was to lighten the taxes and regulations affecting themselves. On 99 percent of issues, the legislators might vote as they wished.

In most states, industries and interest groups—or their agents—provide campaign funds, entertainment, living expenses, and money for special needs. In return, they get access to the men who fix state budgets, set taxes, let contracts, plan highway policies, and work out regulations that affect their own business.

A striking example of pressures by rival interests was provided a few years ago by a battle between railroads and truckers in Pennsylvania.

The Pennsylvania Truckers Association launched a campaign to repeal the weight limits on loads that trucks could carry on state highways. Lobbyists for the truckers descended on the state capitol at Harrisburg. They reminded members of the legislature that the truckers were local businessmen, widely dispersed across the state, and that their money would be thrown into the next campaign to elect a legislature. In local communities, members of the truckers' association demanded action by their legislative spokesmen. The association collected $76,000 from members and distributed the money in about equal sums between candidates of the two political parties. In their local neighborhoods, truckers went out to work for the candidates of their choice.

To counter this campaign, the Pennsylvania railroad and its friends among the eastern railroads mounted a public relations campaign. The railroads did not have members strewn across the state, as did the truckers. Railroad workers were not independent businessmen. They could not develop the kind of help in local communities that the truckers could give to candidates. But the railroads had money.

An annual retainer of $75,000 was paid to a public relations firm for a massive campaign to block the legislation. The railroads also paid the full costs of all advertisements, publicity, and workers. At the end of a year, $274,000, plus the retainer, had gone into the project. The firm put 160 public relations people to work on the project and enlisted the support of the Pennsylvania CIO, the State Federation of Women's Clubs, the Automobile Club, the Pennsylvania Grange, and the State Association of Township Supervisors. Articles, advertisements, and pictures were spread across the state depicting trucks as dangerous road hogs that damaged roads and cost taxpayers money.

In the end, it was pressure from the local truckers and the money they put into the campaigns of candidates for the legislature that paid off. The legislature passed the measure. The governor vetoed it. The legislature passed it again, and the next governor signed it.

The influence "business" had taken two new turns in recent years.

In the 1950s a congressional committee reported that fewer personal contacts were being made by lobbyists. Instead, they were trying to shape opinion back home in the congressional districts and have voters prod members of Congress with letters, telegrams, and personal appeals.

In the 1960s, with campaign costs rising steadily, more emphasis was being placed on picking candidates early and backing them with money through primaries and general elections. Talent scouts searched for candidates whom they thought might be both popular and manageable.

These forms of pressure, being more sophisticated and less visible, may be indirect, but they can prove just as effective as the old fashioned direct methods. They leave the candidate who seeks election or reelection in the uncomfortable position of having to pay tribute to those special interests which have acquired the power to deny him the office he seeks.

CHAPTER FOUR / **The Seamy Side**

In the popular mind, a stigma is attached to the word
"politics"—not without reason. It is said that power corrupts.
It might also be said that the pursuit of power likewise corrupts. With the fruits of electoral victory so rich, men have
been known to toss law and morality to the winds in pursuit
of their objective. They have resorted to corruption and even
violence to insure that the "right" results emerge from the
ballot box. Ties between gangsters and politicians frequently
are exposed by the press. Businessmen and labor unions
occasionally overstep the limits of the Corrupt Practices Act
and find themselves in trouble. And in the process of bringing
a candidate to power, sponsors do not hesitate to treat him as
if he were a box of soap, a tube of toothpaste, or a package of
cigarettes, employing the same kind of electronic merchandising techniques as have been evolved in marketing these
products.

When men invest $1 million or more in a candidate, they
insist on professional planning to insure a return on their investment. A few statistics indicate the kind of help they secure.

In one five-year period, 131 public relations firms were
used in 271 primary campaigns; 151 firms were used in 283

general election campaigns; 77 firms took over the complete management of 183 campaigns. The contests covered nearly every elective office. The broadest use of such agencies was found in California, Illinois, Michigan, New York, Ohio, and Pennsylvania.

A public relations service can arrange anything from radio and television advertising to mapping plans for an entire campaign. More than fifty proefssional campaign managers and pollsters have gone into business around the nation, and the demand for their services is increasing. Most form contacts with the politicians of one party and work regularly for them. About one in every five will sell their services to candidates of either political party.

Morals and ethics play no part in this new political approach. The formula is to take plenty of money and a malleable personality, attack adroitly with the proper amount of television exposure and other advertising, and you have a winner. A good man with brains and morals, but without this professional handling, can be sunk. With it, a secondrater, out for personal glory and profit, can win election.

A few professional managers have won such a reputation that they can command full control of the spending for a candidate's campaign. They make all major campaign decisions and shape the issues. These managers plot an election drive as they would any commercial sales campaign. They use opinion polls to point the way, and shape the candidate's position on issues in a direction that their research indicates will appeal to the greatest number of people.

Now and then, one of them forgets that even a product advertising campaign must be supplemented at the local level by stores; that advertising cannot carry the whole load. In the same way, a candidate cannot overlook his local leaders in the counties and the precincts.

One of the first steps in preparing a campaign is to make a careful study of the opponent's record, searching especially for anything he may have said or done that might tarnish his image.

In large part, this grows out of a conviction that elections are not really won on important issues, but because voters dislike the opposition candidate. It is the image of the hero battling the villain, the good guy over the bad guy. It is cowboys and Indians all over again.

This fiction appears at all levels of politics. In presidential campaigns, Alfred E. Smith and John F. Kennedy were depicted as men who might establish a pipeline to the Vatican. That one of these men lost such a campaign, and the other won is a mark of changing times.

In the past, before Negroes had begun to achieve civil rights and had become a possible political asset in some parts of the country, association with blacks occasionally was exploited in an attempt to damage a political opponent. For example, Claude Pepper of Florida, running for reelection as senator in 1950, found that pictures of himself shaking hands with Negroes had been broadcast across the state. Warren G. Harding was described in a whispering campaign as a man with Negro blood in his heritage.

Other kinds of tricks were also used to "smear" political opponents. There were efforts to bind Harry Truman to the chariot of Tom Pendergast, the Kansas City boss. Lyndon Johnson met disclosures that some of his aides had been involved in improper activities. Senator Millard Tydings of Maryland was confronted with fake campaign pictures showing him in conversation with a Communist leader. No one knows how effective such charges are in changing votes, but they emerge repeatedly.

Devious efforts to swing elections are a part of the whole process. They take different forms from state to state.

In some states and cities, there is a practice of distributing among party workers what is called "walking-around" money. This usually comes from the party's state committee. Baltimore city has long used this practice. Though the custom was outlawed by the Maryland legislature in 1965, it was reinstated in 1968 at the urging of legislators from that city.

The money was supposed to be used to pay drivers and

poll watchers for their services. But no realistic accounting was made of who got how much money for what. In the 1968 election, $95,000 of one party's funds went into Baltimore under this label. All of it was paid out on election day or just before. One party politician was sharply critical of the practice: "In Baltimore, we pay people for doing what citizens in other areas do for nothing."

In another big city, a top-level politician said it cost from $350,000 to $1,000,000 to run a city-wide campaign. He outlined the manner in which his party works:

> Books are put into the hands of each precinct leader giving the name of every person in the area who is not registered. He is told that what he gets from the party in the way of patronage depends on getting his people registered.
>
> As we come to election day, it is good to pass out some reminders. People are informed that there are regulating powers the city can use. Trash collectors can find that rubbish is not tied up properly. There are building inspections. A business man may have to put in new plumbing, new exits, do all sorts of things to meet building and fire inspection. It is pretty nice for him to know someone in the precinct who can take the matter to the top and ask them to "lay off."
>
> At election time, we spend from $150 to $300 for each precinct. This is for car hire and poll-watchers. There usually is a team of six at each polling place. Voters are checked as they come to the polls. We go after those who don't show up.

In national as well as state elections, this city rarely fails to follow the direction of its party leaders.

Naive candidates going into the field for the first time, trying to perform as they believe professionals do, often fall prey to sharpsters. People show up at campaign headquarters and offer to work among their friends if the candidate will provide from $50 to $100 for gasoline money. Many of these people donate their services to several candidates, all on the same terms.

Politicians do not view kindly those who pry into the sources of campaign funds. This goes double when there are questions about any linkage between public officials and criminals. Senator Estes Kefauver of Tennessee discovered this in the 1950s when he paraded some of the nation's most notorious criminals before television cameras and showed that some of them were very friendly with well-placed public officials.

Not since the Kefauver hearings has there been much effort to follow up the leads uncovered then. Only an occasional fleeting glimpse suggests there may be more fire in the ashes than people are willing to acknowledge. A few points uncovered by the Kefauver Committee were:

• A service that provided racing news for illegal bookmakers and gamblers paid $600,000 in political contributions over a three-year period.

• A Chicago and Miami operator of race tracks, closely associated with gang operations, gave $100,000 for the campaign of a candidate for governor of Florida.

• Clear links were established between criminals and politicians in New Orleans, Tampa, California, Illinois and New York.

At least one United States senator left politics after the hearings. A few other politicians disappeared from the lower ranks. But no one has any reason to believe all such connections have been wiped out.

Most of the ties between the underworld and politics are buried in the wards and precincts of big cities. Campaign gifts to candidates, special committees, and campaign organizations run high. One estimate is that as much as 15 percent of the spending at state and local levels comes from underworld sources. Some of this goes through regular campaign committees. A far larger share is recorded in such a manner as to conceal the source.

Virgil W. Peterson, long-time director of the Chicago Crime Commission, once said: "In virtually every section of the country, the underworld has become part and parcel of political organizations that rule over cities and sometimes states." He said ward politicians who make up a slate of candidates often need money and campaign workers, and they get both from the underworld. Honest as well as dishonest public officials win election through their support.

Mobsters, dealing largely in narcotics and gambling, play politics to win protection from politicians for themselves, their people, and their enterprises. They pour money into campaign funds and write it off as a business expense.

Warren Moscow, who knows much about the inner workings of New York city politics, reports that the influence of Frank Costello, and Thomas Luchese on the political operations there did not wane until after 1965.[1] During the same period, Joe Adonis, another gangster, was powerful in King's county.

Outside the New York area, there were clear signs of mob rule in parts of Arkansas, Illinois, Massachusetts, and Missouri.

Now and then a case comes to light that stirs curiosity. In February, 1969, there was a political explosion in Woodbridge, N.J. The president of the municipal council, two business executives and three corporations were found guilty of passing around $110,000. A jury called the money a bribe of the local official. A defense attorney said it was "political money." At stake for the companies were building permits and rights-of-way for a pipeline.

A New Jersey state senator, speaking in defense of the council president, said:

> Elections in this nation are run with cash in every municipality, in every county and everywhere along the line. . . . There is nothing in the law that says a man can't receive a contribution, a political party can't receive

[1] Moscow, Warren. *What Have You Done For Me Lately.* Prentice-Hall, Inc., Englewood Cliffs, N. J., 1967, page 177.

a contribution. . . . How do you think campaigns are run? Did you ever try to hire a poll worker or a car or get a baby-sitter for somebody to go out and vote and think you can pay them with a check on election day?

Every political party must have someone in it who has the capacity to raise money. . . . Now this is an oil company coming through. He [the council president] has to raise money either by going around and sandbagging local people to get it or [play] a one-shot deal with some asset that is coming through.

A special attorney for the Justice Department prosecuting the case did not see it that way. He said: "Rarely if ever has the United States been able . . . to display . . . the kind of naked corruption that we have displayed in this case. . . . Corrupt public officials met and joined . . . big businessmen who were equally corrupt."

Politics in Chicago has never been noted for its loving-kindness. The name of the party in power makes little difference.

In 1903, when Democrats were in power, Lincoln Steffens wrote that reformers could pick up some pointers from Chicago. He called the city: "First in violence, deepest in dirt, lawless, unlovely, ill-smelling, irreverent, news; an overgrown gawk of a — village, the 'tough' among cities, a spectacle for the nation." *Shame of the Cities.*

In 1927, when William Hale Thompson, a Republican, won his last term as mayor, the Chicago Crime Commission estimated that Al Capone and other gangsters put more than $300,000 into the Thompson Campaign. Lloyd Wendt and Herman Kogan described the election day of that year as fairly quiet. They added:

In the early hours two Democratic precinct clubs on the North Side were bombed, two election judges were kidnapped and beaten, half a dozen voters were driven from the polls by pistol-waving thugs and five shots were fired into a West Side polling booth. Little violence occurred during the rest of the day, with police squads cruising the city, machine guns in their laps and tear bombs in their pockets.[2]

With this background in mind, it might be said that John Patrick Tully got off easy in 1968 when he ran for alderman against the hand-picked choice of Mayor Richard Daley's Democratic machine.

Mr. Tully, 33, had lived most of his life in the 14th ward which stands adjacent to the home grounds of Mayor Daley. When Alderman Joe Burke died, Mr. Tully decided to run for that post. His opponent, it turned out, was Edward Burke, 25, son of the former alderman. Both were Democrats, but Mr. Burke had the blessing of the city organization. Mr. Tully ran as an independent.

Back of Mr. Tully were some volunteers, a flimsy scattering of Republicans, the endorsement of the Better Government Association, the *Chicago Sun-Times*, and the *Chicago Daily News*.

Mr. Tully had a small real estate business. He dug into his saving and put $5,000 into the campaign. He lost another $4,000 by taking time from his work during the campaign. Supporters chipped in $1,500 in small contributions. He shook hands, campaigned hard, told his story throughout the ward.

Mr. Burke filled the ward with billboards, signs, leaflets, and newspaper advertisements. His picture went into the windows of many residences—at a profit of $5 to $10 to their owners.

Local citizens, whose names appeared on Tully campaign committee letterheads, got anonymous telephone calls at night. The calls were not from well-wishers.

William H. Rentschler in his column, "Viewpoint from Mid-America," dated March 22, 1969, reported that things got

---

[2] Wendt, Lloyd, and Kogan, Herman. *Big Bill of Chicago*. Indianapolis: Bobbs-Merrill Co., 1953. p. 271.

rough before the campaign entered its final stages. A few items listed were:

• Lugs were removed from the front wheels of a car driven by a Tully volunteer. It had been parked in front of a tavern frequented by workers for the opposition.

• Tully volunteers, distributing posters and literature, had their car bombarded by bricks thrown from the top of a building that was plastered with Burke signs. One of the women volunteers in the car telephoned her husband. He came with a camera and was hit on the leg with a brick. Police showed no interest in the incident.

• A student teacher, passing out Tully literature, was chased by an automobile. Two men got out, seized her by the arm, took her brochures and ordered her to stop her activities or suffer the consequences. She said one of the men was Mr. Burke, the opposition candidate for alderman.

• A hardware store proprietor put a sign supporting Mr. Tully on his building. He got threatening telephone calls demanding that the sign be removed or "we'll close your store for good." The man took down the sign.

• Men on the Democratic payroll in adjacent wards were ordered into the 14th to make sure that Mr. Burke got all the help he needed in the final days of the campaign. City workers came in to trim trees, clean streets, paint street lines and do the normal house-keeping chores cities are supposed to provide.

• On election day, Edward Burke won. Jack Tully said: "The ward organization bought and stole with its usual efficiency."

The incidents occurred in a simple skirmish between members of the same political party. The difference was that Edward Burke had the support of the machine.

It has been thirty years since a famous politician said of a friend: "He wouldn't steal anything except a vote." The statement was made in jest and was taken as such. But at about that time, in the late 1930s, Maurice M. Milligan, a district attorney who refused to obey the overlords of his party in

Missouri, was cracking the Tom Pendergast maching in Kansas city, revealing how a group of unscrupulous men had been winning election after election and perpetuating themselves in power.

No one knows how much money went into the coffers of that machine. One audit showed $68 million diverted from city funds in one way or another. The number of persons on city payrolls was about double the number of actual workers. Most city and county employees had from two to eight false names on registration books under which they could vote in elections. In many precincts, voter registration was larger than the total population. Vacant lots were listed as residences for thousands of names. Some small houses accounted for a hundred or more names of voters. The total registration suggested a city population 200,000 larger than it was.

By the time Mr. Milligan had finished, he had brought 278 persons to trial in federal courts, 259 of whom were convicted. Federal jurisdiction was established because the elections involved federal officials.

There have been many changes in election procedures in recent years. Throughout most of the United States campaigns and elections now move quietly. There is little vote-stealing. Party and election officials are relatively honest. In thousands of voting precincts only one party is represented among the poll watchers. The opposition depends on the integrity of these men and women for an honest count. Usually they get it.

Except for boss-ridden precincts in inner cities and isolated rural areas, a more alert citizenry and constant pressures for faster election returns have trimmed the opportunities for vote frauds. But the chances for fraud still exist. Scurrilous operators remain on the political landscape. They will disappear only if and when an alert electorate completes the work of reform.

CHAPTER FIVE

/ **Organizing for Power**

Political parties are the instruments used by men and groups to win control of government. The parties mesh with government at every level. They produce candidates for every job.

According to one estimate, there are a million offices to which men are elected in the United States. However, no accurate count of all officeholders has ever been made. If the figure of the International City Managers' Association for the early 1960s is adjusted upward for growth, the number of governmental units in the nation comes to about 95,000. This covers federal, state, county, and city governments plus a wide variety of special agencies ranging from those that run schools, libraries, soil conservation districts, and flood control districts down to special categories in some states that run cemeteries. There are about 55,000 of these special districts.

An attempt to determine the number of elective officials for these units, especially below the statewide level, leads to a maze. Not all cities reply to questionnaires from city manager groups. The National Association of Counties has little information about the number of county officials. The same is true about the special agencies.

In 1970, normal procedure calls for the election of 468 U.S.

senators and representatives. This covers the 35 senators and 435 representatives whose terms expire. At the state level, 35 governors and 357 other officials are to be elected on a statewide basis. With them are to be chosen 6,403 members of state legislatures and the officeholders in 2,017 of the 3,043 counties.

For 1972, as in each leap year, the same number of federal officials are to be selected—468—plus a president and vice president. Twenty-two states choose governors and 284 other statewide officials. At the lower levels, 6,066 members of state legislatures will be elected along with officials in 1,444 counties.

Sprinkled along the way at different dates are a variety of other elections. Kentucky, Mississippi, New Jersey, and Virginia elect governors and state and county officials in odd-numbered years. The same practice is followed by some 36,000 cities and townships.

If these figures do not seem to jibe, particularly with respect to the number of senators and governors, it should be recalled that in 1974—as in each third even-numbered election year—thirty-four senators will be elected. At the governorship level, ten states still elect state and county officials for two-year terms. In most states, county officials are chosen in the same elections as governors and other statewide officials.

However many elective offices may be represented in this mass of governmental machinery—probably between 750,000 and 1,000,000—the political parties are prepared to produce at least one man, and usually two men, for each job. Jobs and power are the red and white corpuscles that make up the lifeblood of political parties.

Parties are created to elect their members to office. To do this, politicians must achieve two things: produce candidates and issues that will stir interest and win votes; and keep open the lines to important contributors of money and services. In simplest terms, these are the real functions of political parties.

The United States is said to have a two-party system.

Voters, even writers who should know better, speak of the national Democratic and Republican parties as 2 distinctive entities. Actually, there are 100 separate parties, two in each state. The Democratic party in Georgia or Louisiana bears little resemblance to the Democratic party in Massachusetts or Illinois. Republicans of New York and Pennsylvania might feel ill at ease among the people of their own party in Kansas or Nebraska.

Party diversity does not stop at the differences between parties bearing the same label. The chances are, in virtually every state, you find two or more factions fighting for control of each party. Sometimes the struggle becomes so intense that a fragment will break away and start a separate party. The Liberal party in New York began as an American Labor party; it was set up as a shelter under which organized workers could gather to support Franklin D. Roosevelt. The Conservative party in the same state was formed years later by Republicans who regarded Nelson Rockefeller as too "liberal." The Progressives who followed the late Robert M. LaFollette in Wisconsin are now divided between the Democratic and Republican parties. In Minnesota, there is still active feuding between the old Farm Laborites and the Democrats as they try to work under the same tent.

This diversity often is reflected in the membership of the national committees of the two parties. It would be hard to imagine two points of view more different than those of Eugene B. Connor of Alabama and Mrs. Vel Phillips of Wisconsin. Mr. Connor as chief of the police department in Birmingham used trained dogs and fire hoses against civil rights demonstrators. Mrs. Phillips, a chic, attractive Negro lawyer from Milwaukee, member of the city council, herself took part in civil rights demonstrations in her home city. Mrs. Phillips and Mr. Connor were spokesmen for their respective states on the Democratic National Committee at the same time in the early 1960s.

During the same period, a professional staff member of the Republican National Committee attended a regional party meeting in Atlanta. He was upset when he emerged from a closed session where he had been listening to a report by the Mississippi state chairman of his party. The staff member said: "He [the Mississippian] bragged that the Republicans in his state had just succeeded in removing from office the last remaining Negro county chairman. There goes our hope for winning Negro votes in the South. Time was when that was about all we had in Mississippi."

These differences illustrate the patchwork of ideas and people who speak for the 100 separate parties at the upper levels of the political hierarchy. At this level in both parties, policies and programs are debated with the intent to bind together a majority of the dominant party factions in most of the states. Many of these upper level party people are non-officeholders. This little band is invisible to the average voter. Unless the voter is a big contributor, he may have little influence on the selection of a member of the national committee from his state.

The national committee is the keystone of the political structure. Its members are either political professionals or amateurs who know where campaign funds are buried. Below the national committee are the 100 state committees of the two major parties. Each of these is a separate entity to be dealt with by national politicians. George Wallace, for instance, called himself an Alabama Democrat and dominated party politics in his state even though he denounced in bitter terms the national Democratic party.

A man and a woman from each state and the District of Columbia are chosen as members of the two national committees. Selections are made in presidential election years either in state party conventions or by the state delegations to the national conventions at which presidential and vice presidential candidates are nominated. During the four years between conventions, the committee is empowered to act for the party. Members of the committees, since they are chosen during factional fights for the presidential nomination, usually reflect the views of the dominant faction in their states. If these views happen to differ from those of the person who wins the nomination, we are likely to hear little about them. Committee members are dedicated party people. Moreover, there is the matter of patronage to be considered if the party's candidate wins the White House.

Much of the work of the national committees is done by highly skilled professionals. These men and women stay in their jobs year in and year out, regardless of the fortunes of the party on the national scene. Their value increases with experience. They collect and analyze election statistics, look for soft spots in the opposition party, write speeches and party publications, handle press relations, keep in touch with party people throughout the states, provide speakers for fund-raising affairs, and keep open the pipelines through which the money flows to maintain their operations. Professionals, little known outside their own fields, do the real work of running the national committees, as well as the senatorial and congressional campaign committees of their parties. The latter two are operated as separate units.

Often, the chairmanship of a national committee is a figurehead job, especially if the party does not hold the White House. When the party is in control of the White House, the national chairman usually is one of the clearing agents for federal jobs. Only when a solid professional such as James A. Farley and Lawrence O'Brien for the Democrats and Leonard Hall and Ray Bliss for the Republicans is in the post does a national chairman accomplish much. However, John M. Bailey of Connecticut, an experienced professional, found his hands tied as Democratic chairman because President Lyndon Johnson had little faith in committee operations.

Meanwhile, Ray Bliss was putting together a Republican machine that lifted Richard M. Nixon into the presidency. He ignored issues and personalities and emphasized organization, impressing this policy on state chairmen and leaders in big cities, counties, small cities, and suburban areas. Two reasons lay behind his work.

First, he had to bind together enough of the fifty state

leaders of his party to win an election. In the end, this is what a national victory of one of the major parties boils down to. A majority of the state party bosses must be convinced that it is to their interest to put aside factional differences and go out and fight for a given candidate. Very few Republicans had done this in 1964, however much lip service they may have given to Barry Goldwater.

Next, Mr. Bliss had to teach his people the basic rules of politics. With all the good will in the world, state and local leaders cannot win an election unless they have the know-how. And in all the talk about new politics in recent years, many politicians forgot the first few letters of the political alphabet. What Mr. Bliss told his people, in essence, was this:

- Recruit good candidates.
- Develop issues that hit home to the voters in your community.
- Raise plenty of money.
- Broaden the party base by bringing in young workers, developing ties with teachers and professors, reaching out for ethnic and minority groups.
- Build registration.
- Set vote quotas and insist that precinct captains meet them.

This exemplifies the work of a national chairman at a high level of efficiency. Mr. Bliss ignored primary fights in the states and the rivalry of candidates for the presidential nomination. His dominant purpose was to get party people to work together in their own states after the intraparty battles were over. His work was not the kind that drew headlines or put his face on the television screens. He called himself a "nuts and bolts" man.

The work was of such a high order that Mr. Bliss remained as chairman during Mr. Nixon's presidential campaign, a rather unusual procedure. In most campaigns, the presidential candidate puts his own man in the national chairmanship after the nominating convention. Barry Goldwater put Dean Burch into the chairmanship and sprinkled his own people, many of them inexperienced, through key committee spots in 1964. Hubert Humphrey, after winning the Democratic nomination in 1968, persuaded the highly skilled Lawrence F. O'Brien to take the chairmanship and direct his campaign. But the factional disputes among the fifty Democratic parties were of such a nature that one could hardly have developed in two months a working agreement with enough state bosses to win an election. The agreements Mr. Bliss had worked out during a four-year period were strong enough to remain in place through an election.

When the voting was done and Mr. Nixon was installed in the White House, Mr. Bliss left the national committee before federal jobs were passed around to the faithful. He had been exceptionally impartial as national chairman. Working for a party victory, he had not closely identified himself with the winning candidate. He knew nothing of the private bargains that had been made with varying factions in the states to help the candidate win the nomination. Those who did were the people who now had first claim on jobs at the disposal of the new president. Rogers C. B. Morton of Maryland, Mr. Nixon's floor manager at the Miami convention, a man who had been involved in the dickering for delegate support, knew the men who had worked hardest and had given the most to help Mr. Nixon win nomination and election. He was installed in Mr. Bliss's place.

This was not an unusual move by Mr. Nixon. Many presidents had done it before. They recognized that a change in administration in the White House brings a realignment of party forces in the states. The faction that did not support the winning candidate has little or nothing to say about who gets the federal jobs in their state. Even though it may be the dominant faction in the state and may name the national committeeman, federal patronage moves through other channels—a governor, a senator, the leader of the faction that did support the winner. If the ruling faction in the state supported the winning candidate, however, normal procedure gives the national committeeman a voice in deciding to whom the job will go. National committeemen, though less well known than senators or governors, sometimes speak with more authority in the top councils of the party. Unlike the senator or governor, the voter has nothing to say about the choice of a national committeeman.

Similarly, the voter has no influence on the selection of the state chairman of his party. This man runs party affairs in his state and is occasionally made a member of the National Committee. Often, he speaks with more authority about the conduct of state party affairs than does the national committeeman. He directs statewide campaigns, knows the county chairmen, and helps them in their work.

The state chairman usually is elected by members of the state party committee. The committee may pick him for his ability as a political manager. Or he may be simply a figurehead, chosen because he is acceptable to leaders of opposing factions in the party. Again, he may be handpicked by the governor, a senator, or a group of powerful men behind the scenes.

Highly important to the work of the state chairman and his committee is the efficiency of the finance committee, or money-raisers, who must turn up funds for statewide campaigns along with the state quota allocated by the national committee to help keep the national mechanism running. Sometimes the finance committee is an official group, headed by a chairman; again, it may be a wholly informal cluster of men and women who know how to tap the finances of people interested in the party or who want to get things from its elected officials.

Headquarters for the state committee and the principal office for the state chairman usually are in the state capital, with additional offices in the principal cities of the state. Standard equipment for these offices is a mimeograph machine, a list of registered voters, and heaps of campaign literature. Usually, there is a full-time executive director whose job is to keep in contact with party officials around the state.

In active two-party states, a publicity man writes a publication for the faithful and provides a flow of propaganda for newspapers.

The state party is an independent unit. It is the tool of that state's ruling faction and its relations with the national party are only as close as the ruling faction in the state wishes them to be. It builds registration and promotes the campaigns of candidates for governor and statewide offices. County and city officials tie the local henchmen into the party at the local level. Except in name, the state party often has little or nothing to do with races for the United States Senate and House of Representatives. Many members of Congress report that they receive no help of any kind from their state party committees. This lack of support for federal officeholders tends to widen the gap between the 100 state parties and the two national parties.

State committees vary in size and in mode of operation. There is no common denominator. Each state draws up the rules for recognition and operation of a party. Since the rules are written by politicians in state legislatures, they are drawn to fit the needs of local politicians. A party must have a minimum number of voters to get its candidates on the ballot. Once it has the required number, it usually has fairly wide latitude in setting the rules for the selection of candidates. It may do this either in convention or in primaries. It may fix its own organizational structure.

In each state, the major parties have an overall group that comprises the state committee under one name or another. Rules under which these groups operate vary widely and often are changed. Neither the Republican nor the Democratic National Committee has an up-to-date compilation of the working procedures of the 100 separate parties they call their own. The most recent study was done by the National Municipal League in 1967.

The size of state committees ranges from 14 (in Iowa)—to 972 for Democrats, and up to 1,262 for Republicans (in California). In at least thirteen states, the committees consist of more than 200 members, too many to make decisions easily or to meet often. The committees are supposed to select their own chairmen, but more often these men are thrust upon the groups by a state official or an important group within the party. No ordinary voter can project his voice into this back-room procedure. Even in the selection of members of the state committees, registered voters are given a choice in only a dozen states. Party people make most of these decisions at the county level.

The county leader, or county chairman, is an important party post in all well-organized states. Here again, in most states, the average voter has no influence in choosing him. He is picked by faithful party workers even in the thirty-odd states that permit registered voters to cast ballots for members of the county committees.

For example, in Pennsylvania the size of the county committees ranges from 20 members in Cameron County to 2,566 in Allegheny County, which holds Pittsburgh. In each election district, or precinct, the voters elect leaders who serve as members of the county committee. As a group, the district leaders assemble and choose a county chairman. With some variations, this is the practice followed in most states that allow voters to have any part in electing party officials.

The county chairman often has more power than many county officials whose names are on the ballot. He is a guardian of party affairs in his county and spokesman for ward and precinct people who want jobs for party workers. If his own party happens to hold the principal offices in the county, these jobs may run from judgeships or important posts in governmental agencies down to minor posts in highway and public works departments. The chairman's effectiveness in getting these jobs has been weakened somewhat by civil service laws, but the operation of civil service is not necessarily immune to outside influence.

In his own county or city, the man who stands at the top of the party organization wangles new sewers, roads, and street lights and arranges for better trash removal and other community services. While civic organizations are discussing a problem in a meeting, the county chairman can walk into the office of a county official and get action. He is one of the small group of politicians in each community who gets things done. Around this group cluster the contractors, real estate men, and store keepers who have paid the campaign expenses and want favors of one kind or another. Little tokens of recognition flow out to others in return for special work they have done on primary and election days. This loosely organized handful of people picks the candidates for the county, controls the primaries, and provides the men to be voted into office.

Just as state chairmen and national committeemen wield great power in national conventions, so county chairmen in populous areas become important in selecting candidates for state offices. To win the presidency, a candidate needs a working agreement with leaders of dominant factions of his party in a large number of states. Similarly, a man who wishes to be governor or United States senator must work out his alliances with the important county leaders in his state. After election, these officials feel obligated to certain important county leaders when making appointments to office, shaping tax and other policies, and handing out contracts. The county leader knows in intimate detail who has helped to finance the campaign and which precinct leaders have turned out the workers to gather the most votes. The county leader's power in his own community and his future advancement in the party grow with his ability to win favors for his own people.

The bottom rung on the political ladder, and often the most important when it comes to winning elections, is the precinct, or district, leader. This is the person the county leader must rely on for success. A precinct leader who wants jobs, contracts, or other political favors will use all of his influence to win the nomination of a man supported by his county or city chairman if he thinks the local leader will have a hand in making decisions after election. And it is the precinct leader who must get people registered and turn out the voters.

The precinct, or district, may be a few square blocks in a city or a few square miles in a rural area. It holds from 400 to 2,000 voters. In 1968, there were about 168,000 precincts in the United States called by various names in different states. The average precinct or division holds 600 to 700 voters.

Often the precinct leader is the only party official whose name is presented to the voters in an election. This is a choice made in a party primary, not in a general election. To the voters, it sounds like an unimportant post. Usually, the name is unfamiliar to them. They either mark their ballot without knowledge of the man or the position, or they fail to vote for this candidate. A precinct leader in Kansas reported that he once was elected by a landslide of one write-in vote, and that on another occasion he squeaked through by a margin of three to two. In any highly organized area, however, there will be plenty of dedicated party people to make certain that their man wins.

A change in the direction of party affairs can occur in these precinct elections so often overlooked by the average citizen. In the 1950s, Carmine DeSapio was the top Democrat in New York County and national committeeman for his state. As such, he had a voice in national politics. His county post grew out of the fact that he had been elected leader of his district. A rival faction attacked Mr. DeSapio at the local level, and although only a few thousand voted, he was beaten for reelection as district leader. This marked the end of Mr. DeSapio as a national politician. Under New York party rules, only district leaders are eligible for election as county leaders.

At the precinct level, canvassers are enlisted and trained. They are sent out to work their own neighborhoods. They make certain that families are registered to vote, above all, the people of their own party. They circulate campaign literature. They check voters in and out of the polls on election day.

There is nothing new about the process, nor is it out-moded despite demonstrations on college campuses, the pontificating over television, and the books about "new" politics. Electronic communication, computers, and polls are only gadgets that are used to implement the basic methods used in every election since 1800, when Aaron Burr outsmarted Alexander Hamilton, took the electoral votes of New York away from John Adams, and gave them to Thomas Jefferson.

Modern politics in America began at that point. Burr built an organization of young men. He shaped campaign policies in his law office, put down factional fights, developed a popular ticket of candidates, and set up a finance committee whose methods might be used to good effect today. He also made a card index of every voter in the city. It listed the voter's political history, his views, his habits, his temperament, his health, and how much trouble would be involved in getting him to the polls. When computers and opinion polls do the same job today, it is called "new" politics.

The closest approach to the Burr system is that on Chicago's South Side. It made Representative William Levi Dawson the most powerful Negro politician in the United States. But Mr. Dawson only perfected and broadened a system started by Representative Oscar DePriest and used originally for the Republicans when Mayor William (Big Bill) Thompson ruled the city for that party. Mr. Dawson grew up in the DePriest organization and served for six years as a Republican member of the city council. In 1939, Mr. Dawson formed a working friendship with Democratic Mayor Edward J. Kelly and switched parties.

As ward committeeman for the Democrats, Mr. Dawson was inside the ruling councils of the party. He had control over patronage jobs in his ward, decided who would run for alderman, named certain judges, picked delegates to party conventions, and decided who could move ahead in the party. In 1942, Mr. Dawson was elected to the House of Representatives and remained there through the years. His voice was important in Cook County and the Democratic

National Committee. He was chairman of a powerful House committee. And in Chicago, as the Negro population expanded, he extended his powers by installing his own men as committeemen for the party in six wards in addition to his own. By the time Richard J. Daley arrived on the scene, Mr. Dawson and his skilled lieutenants had combined the largest single group of voters in Illinois into a cohesive voting unit. He helped to put Mr. Daley into city hall as mayor.

In Chicago, the strands of power reach down to the precinct. Each precinct has from 500 to 700 voters with its own captain. There are 60 to 100 precincts in each ward. The precinct captain is responsible to the ward committeeman from whom flow jobs and favors from city hall. These go to precinct workers as a reward for getting out the votes. How long a precinct captain remains in his job depends on how well he succeeds in producing votes. This is the way the organization worked under Republican Mayor Thompson. It still works that way under Democratic Mayor Daley.

From the early days of the DePriest organization, ward committeemen have kept a file on their workers. In the precincts, Dawson workers send cards to voters on Mother's Day, at Christmas, and on birthdays. On special occasions, they send flowers. One member makes regular visits to hospitals and to the elderly in nursing homes. Women outnumber men by four to one in the Dawson organization.

A Negro editor who moved into the South Side of Chicago reported that he had hardly settled before he received a call from the precinct captain asking what the new arrival would like. "I asked what was available," said the editor. "The captain said if I had any trouble getting a phone or public utilities, if there was trouble about garbage disposal, or any little thing to let him know."

In Mr. Dawson's own ward, there are sixty-four precincts with twenty workers to the precinct, including the captain. Those who hold jobs with the city, county, or state are required to pay dues to the organization amounting to 2 percent of their salaries. Each precinct is required to be self-sustaining financially. Social affairs are held regularly at head-quarters with admission charges scaled as low as twenty-five cents.

From September to April, regular classes on political organization are held weekly at the Dawson headquarters. Party workers are taught by political science students. The workers are required to attend to learn how to organize voters, how to make themselves known in their area, and how to serve the needs of voters. As a class project, fifty workers assembled in a twenty-story apartment complex and canvassed it completely in twenty-nine minutes. The building is a precinct within itself. The crew of party workers were required to bring back the answers to questions they had been supplied with. It is standard practice in the Dawson organization to cover a building of this kind within twenty-four hours.

The Dawson organization is unique in American politics. Under Mayor Thompson, so many Negroes got jobs at the city hall that it was called "Uncle Tom's Cabin." Democrats gave Negroes a greater role in the power politics of the city. Unlike political machines that once ruled other big cities, the Dawson organization did not crumble under the impact of the New Deal and numerous forms of welfare. Instead, it became a channel through which citizens could get city, state, and federal help. It offers advice and help to voters who do not know how to get through the red tape. Without such help, many South Side residents would not know how to get welfare payments, unemployment insurance, social security, and, often, jobs.

Mr. Dawson is now a tired old man, yet no successor to this key politician is in sight.

A point often emphasized in the Chicago operation is that elections are won by organizations that make politics a full-time business. The workers keep in close touch with the voters. They raise money in small amounts regularly and they always try to broaden the base of financial support on the theory that interest in the success of the party mounts as donors multiply.

Outside the cities, few states have a party organization that reaches down to the precinct level. In rural areas, the organization often stops at the county seat. Frequently, the party structure is only a paper affair—a list of names of persons who have no power and little interest and do little work.

In almost twenty states, the average voter has no voice in choosing party officials at any level. Here, politics is in the hands of those who hope to gain power or profit from their work. They choose their own precinct or county leaders and ratify the choices at party rallies that the voter rarely knows about or bothers to attend if he is aware of them.

Fewer than 3 percent of the voters take enough interest in party affairs to attend precinct meetings or county rallies at which delegates are chosen for state conventions. The work of a party may be done at a precinct meeting by half a dozen, or fewer, persons. In one case, a man and his wife chose each other to represent their precinct at a county meeting. In another, five persons showed up for a county rally. Four of them belonged to an opposition wing of the party. The fifth was a member of the state's dominant faction and had been designated as temporary chairman. He banged the gavel for order, nominated himself as permanent chairman, and declared the nominations closed and himself elected. He did the same in electing himself to the state convention. The four opponents roared their frustration, but he got away with it and was seated over their protests at the convention.

Abuse of this kind is the price the public must pay for a dormant electorate.

CHAPTER SIX / **Financing Campaigns**

Campaign spending is now so lavish that it exceeds our ability to keep track of it. Money flows out in all directions. Even the fairly sketchy reports to the clerk of the House of Representatives for the 1968 campaign have not been analyzed. One agency that did this work in the past looked at the bundles of material and threw up its collective hands in despair. As a result, there is only a very general idea of what happened to the millions of dollars that were spent.

To the voter, looking on from the outside, the most obvious expenses are those that involve television, radio, newspaper and billboard advertising, and the cost of hauling candidates from place to place for meetings and rallies. These can be seen by everyone. They cost millions of dollars, and the prices are rising daily.

The cost of half an hour of network television during the evening hours when it will reach the largest audience is $96,000. For one hour with a few advance notices and a little money spent on production, the cost can easily be to $250,000. A local candidate on a first-class metropolitan station will pay a minimum of $1,250 for a half hour of "prime" time.

In a statewide campaign, a candidate can be assessed up to

$200 an hour for the lease of an airplane to shuttle him from place to place. The cost of a jet for presidential candidates requires real money. Newsmen accompanying the candidate pay first class fare on a mileage basis for the trip.

Behind the scenes are a host of activities never seen by the voter. Almost every candidate tries to soften up the newsmen by providing free food and drinks on the plane. Advance men travel ahead of the party to arrange for tumultuous receptions at airports. Other staff members stay behind to report to the campaign managers how much impact the candidate made on his audience.

The modern campaign staff includes speech, song, and jingle writers, stage directors, pollsters, advance men, statistical researchers, precinct bosses, leaders of interest groups, public relations advisers, contributors, solicitors, finance chairmen, field representatives, accountants, confidential friends, advisors on a wide variety of special subjects, leaders of women's groups, and specialists in dealing with ethnic groups. They produce and distribute tons of literature, badges, and gifts.

Skimming down the list of one candidate's expenses, we find these items: pay to a modeling agency for pretty girls to be displayed at campaign rallies; radio, television, newspaper, and billboard advertising; rent for campaign headquarters; electricity; telephones; telegrams; automobile rental; small airplanes at $200 an hour; airplane tickets; registration drives; hillbilly bands; public relations counsel; writers; printing and distribution costs for campaign literature; rental of an elephant; comic books; sample ballots; gifts to college funds and relief associations; a traffic ticket; convention liquor; corsages.

Instead of cash contributions, many companies lend their favorite candidates the use of billboards, office furniture and equipment, mailing lists, airplanes, or stamp meters. They sometimes pay for advertising, publish yearbooks, or lend public relations people, lawyers, and secretaries.

As campaigns grow more costly, professional campaigners are going into business in many states. They conduct polls or run a complete campaign for the candidate, using television, computers, and other modern devices. With each new gadget, costs increase.

It is difficult to determine how much and where campaign money is wasted. Most politicians agree that too much money is spent. Yet they are uncertain how costs might be cut. One professional who has worked in many campaigns said: "The amount of money spent in politics is completely indecent. One half of the money is wasted, but you don't know which half."

It is anyone's guess how much money will be spent in 1970 to elect sixty-eight senators and governors. There are at least a dozen states in which the smallest price for election to one of these offices is a million dollars. With opposing candidates spending about the same amount to lose the election, the total becomes doubly impressive.

Perhaps the most expensive campaign of recent years was the 1966 campaign of Nelson Rockefeller for reelection as governor of New York. Polling and preparation began more than a year in advance. On the basis of official figures, Mr. Rockefeller put almost $5 million into the campaign. One Democratic estimate was twice that amount. The job pays $50,000 a year—1 percent of Mr. Rockefeller's estimated investment in the campaign.

The governor's researchers worked out detailed listings of what each county in the state had received in the way of roads, bridges, and scholarships. They estimated how high property taxes would have gone in each area if there had been no state aid. There were more than 3,000 commercials on 22 television stations and 27 million brochures, buttons, and leaflets. Mr. Rockefeller visited every one of the 62 counties in the state. His campaign headquarters filled 84 rooms in the New York Hilton hotel. He had a paid staff of 307, including the best men available for specific jobs. Each step in the campaign was charted by a poll. All this work and money went into a campaign in which he had no real opposition for his party's nomination.

Often it costs as much or more to win a party's nomination than it does to win or lose the election campaign that follows. In Pennsylvania, Milton Shapp, a Democrat, spent $1.4 million to win his party's nomination for governor and about $1.1 million for the campaign against his Republican opponent, Raymond P. Shafer, who won the election.

The number of states in which a candidate for statewide office must expect to spend as much as a million dollars increases with each election. And a large part of this must be raised by the candidate himself since the resources of his party generally are not available until he has won the nomination.

Accordingly, he taps his friends, college classmates, and business associates. He also uses his own money.

He tries to pick an able finance chairman to handle the money-raising problem. Activities include fund-raising dinners, the sale of campaign emblems, and appeals for money mailed to private homes. Requests also are made on television and radio. Rarely do these appeals for small contributions yield much money. The large sums still must come from big contributors.

Thoughtful politicians are worried about the problem, but no one has yet come up with a workable answer. There have been many proposals. One is that contributions of $25 to $100 be made tax deductible. Another is that the two major parties cooperate in raising funds. A third is that campaigns be financed by the government through tax money, a plan that stirs strong opposition from many citizens. This plan is opposed even more sharply by the back room managers and the political professionals who raise funds. If the power to provide campaign money is taken from them, their control over both the party machinery and the politicians is diminished.

The operation of politics at the national level depends largely on fund-raising in states and local communities. About half the money raised by each of the two parties in campaign years comes through state and local units.

Solicitation of funds from state and local government work-

ers is still widespread in many states where party organization is strong. Employees are assessed a percentage of their
salaries. "Two percent clubs" are not infrequent. Now and
then the assessment may be 5 percent of a month's salary.
This applies to thousands of workers in various state or city
departments. The state party chairman simply asks the department head to solicit his employee for funds.

A study of Democratic financing in Indiana, undertaken
in 1964 by Robert J. McNeill under the joint sponsorship of
Indiana University and the Citizen's Research Foundation,
reported that the "2 percent club," introduced in the 1930s,
had been brought to a higher level of efficiency in the
1960s.

The report said that a collector had been installed in each
state agency to gather employee contributions for each pay
period. The collector kept contribution records for each employee. In addition, some employees were required to give
1 or 2 percent of their income to their county chairmen.

In the interval between the 1930s and 1960s when Republicans were in power in Indiana, the report said, workers
generally were asked to give one week's pay each year to the
Republican state committee. This system applied to about
6,350 workers in the highway, revenue, and administration
departments and the bureau of motor vehicles.

Another glimpse into Indiana campaign financing was provided by a list of assessments on each candidate for statewide
office. These ranged downward from $2,500 for candidates for
the U.S. Senate and for governor. A place on the ticket cost
$2,000 for a supreme court judge; $1,250 for lieutenant governor and appellate judges; $1,000 for attorney general; $750
for secretary of state, auditor, treasurer, and court reporter.
The money went into a common campaign fund.

State and local employees are more vulnerable to solicitations than are federal workers. There is a law against asking
federal workers for campaign contributions. Yet, hardly an
election year passes without reports of such solicitations.
Letters invite workers to attend fund-raising dinners in Wash-

ington and elsewhere. In one instance, Democratic leaders in Kansas sent requests to postmasters and rural carriers in letters to their homes. About half of the postmasters and 13 percent of the carriers responded.

A few years ago, the national committeeman in one state wrote to 500 persons who had been given federal jobs. He asked for $125 to $500 from each, according to the importance of his position, saying that the party needed money to process appointments and to support candidates for Congress and the state legislature. Very few gave what was asked.

Federal workers in general do not contribute to campaigns and are not asked to do so. Some make voluntary contributions—not necessarily to the party in power. One federal worker who entered government service during the Hoover administration stayed through the Roosevelt, Truman, Eisenhower, and Kennedy administrations and retired with a high civil service rating during the Johnson administration without ever contributing to either party. Similar cases are found in many state governments.

Both parties have tried for years to broaden the base of political contributions. Students of politics agree that the system is in danger as long as men in public office can get there only through the help of big contributors, many of whom put a price on their assistance.

Republican fund-raisers are usually successful businessmen, financiers, or their lawyers. They often have records of public service, have raised money for nonpolitical causes, and have ties to the financial leaders of their region who provide a ready-made list of prospective donors.

In the Democratic party, fund-raisers fall into a similar pattern. But Democrats have no ready-made strategy for raising money. Everything is informal and confusing. They get money where they can find it: from the fishing industry in the Northwest; from some oil companies in the Southwest; from insurance companies in the Middle West; from "liberals" in the East.

What It Costs to Become President, Governor, or Member of Congress

President.................... $35 million to $60 million
Governor.................. $50,000 to $5 million
U.S. Senator................ $250,000 to $5 million
U.S. Representative........... $30,000 to $300,000

Note: These figures cover total costs actually paid by different winning candidates, including primary and post-nomination expenditures. In many cases, losing candidates spent equal amounts.
Source: Reported expenditures and published estimates.

The Rising Election Bill

What we spend for national, state and local campaigns
(Millions)

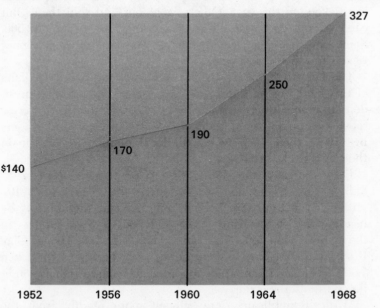

Note: Figures exclude expenditures prior to nomination of candidates. Each annual amount is composed roughly of 15 percent for expenditures at the national level 50 percent at the state level and 35 percent at the local level.
Source: Published statistics and estimates of expenditures by both major parties.

The Democratic national committeeman for each state has a quota he is supposed to meet. He may pass the job along to a senator, a governor, or a businessman. The top responsibility rests with the national treasurer and finance chairman. But plans and operations change from year to year and vary from state to state.

About half of the money for state campaigns of each party is now raised at special dinners where the party faithful, and those whom they can talk into buying tickets, can listen to big-name politicians. Dinners are arranged at all levels from the precinct up, with prices ranging from $10 to $1,000. There are breakfasts, luncheons, teas, coffees, picnics, cocktail parties, and bridge nights.

One state finance chairman organized a dinner with a price tag of $100. He called together forty men and gave each of them twenty-five tickets. A few of the men paid for the tickets on the spot. Others went out and sold them. But each of the forty men was responsible for raising $2,500. Some companies manage to charge the cost of such dinner tickets to expense accounts.

The help that Mr. Nixon gave his party in attending affairs of this kind was an important factor in getting him the presidential nomination. He ate his way back and forth across the nation many times, cementing his ties with local leaders by giving them help where all local politicians need it—in their own back yards.

Between 1964 and 1967, Mr. Nixon raised between $5 million and $6 million for his party by speaking at Republican functions. He helped congressional Republicans by heading a Booster Club in 1966. It raised $1.3 million. In the same campaign, Mr. Nixon helped Mrs. Helen Clay Frick, the Pittsburgh steel heiress, to bestow two dozen $1,000 contributions upon Republican congressional candidates around the country.

While Republicans draw money more readily from the business community, Democrats are more successful in getting money from organized labor.

Files of big Democratic party donors often are held by individual candidates for their own use and are not turned over to the party. Quite a few wealthy men are willing to give money to a Democratic candidate whom they like, but would not make a contribution either to the national or the state Democratic party, nor want their friends to know of their contributions.

This method of individual financing prevents the Democrats from creating a fund-raising group that could function straight down the line from the national level to the states. The splintering of each party into fifty separate state fragments is also a hindrance to Republicans in their financing. But there is a semblance of a system among Republicans.

Republicans have a finance committee that consists of a chairman in each state and twenty-five or more members at large. Some of these members are picked because they give heavily to the party; others, because they are able to persuade their friends to donate. A budget is agreed upon and a quota assigned to each state. Democrats try a similar method but with little success. In the main, the Democratic party organization lives from hand to mouth.

Ohio Republicans have a financial arrangement that has been regarded as a model by other states. Party fund-raisers from various states have been sent to Ohio to study this method. Here, professional fund-raisers work under a paid finance director who assigns men to specific areas of the state.

Aside from the major-party operations, special groups interested in government policies raise money for those candidates whose ideas conform most closely to their own. The money may go to a candidate of either party. These special groups range in ideology from the extreme "right" to the far "left."

More than 1,300 associations representing business, professional, and trade groups have offices in Washington. Most are set up to get something from the federal government or to keep their members well-informed of what the government is doing. In addition, the 200-odd separate branches of labor unions maintain officials in the nation's capital.

The work of labor unions often carries more weight with public officials in producing effective political action—both in Washington and in the country as a whole—than the 1,300 associations mentioned above. Professional and trade associations pick candidates and put cash behind them, but they have had little success in organizing for politics and inducing their members to take an active part.

The U.S. Chamber of Commerce, among other interested groups, has developed a course in practical politics. Its aim is to teach business leaders how to influence local parties and gain a voice in choosing candidates. Various corporations and local chambers of commerce have conducted such courses. Realistic assessments suggest, however, that the results have been small in proportion to the effort.

High-level corporation officials do not care to ring doorbells. If they participate in politics, they want to come in at the top. White-collar workers in the lower echelons of officialdom tend to shy away from politics despite the urgings of their superiors, and local politicians are skeptical about the whole experiment. Politicians figure that the most that can be expected from corporation officials is money, and even this may be split between the two parties. Labor, on the other hand, can produce both money and campaign workers with know-how.

Organized labor played its first important role in politics in the 1936 campaign of Franklin D. Roosevelt for reelection. Reports said the unions spent $750,000 in that campaign—quite a sum for those depression days. It was about eight times the amount the American Federation of Labor had raised for political purposes during the previous thirty years.

By 1943, the Congress of Industrial Organizations had turned to grassroots campaigning to bring sympathetic legislators and executives into office at local, state, and national levels. Its early endeavors were handled through a Political Action Committee (PAC).

Today, AFL-CIO works through a Committee on Political Education. COPE puts money and work into efforts to increase the number of voters and to get them to the polls. It helps candidates with money and trained political workers. It tries to mobilize its members by door-to-door campaigning. It distributes educational and propaganda materials through individual unions.

In one high-pressure campaign for a Senate seat, members of COPE made 60,000 telephone calls, distributed 460,000 pieces of literature and leaflets, and established a central file of 65,000 union members. In addition, it put an unlisted amount of money into the state. All this was done in a state that does not rank among those in which unions are strong. The senator was reelected.

Seventy-seven percent of union members are in seventeen states: California, Illinois, Indiana, Massachusetts, Michigan, Minnesota, Missouri, Montana, Nevada, New Jersey, New York, Ohio, Oregon, Pennsylvania, Washington, West Virginia, and Wisconsin. In these states and in many parts of others where members are concentrated, unions are both feared and respected by politicians. But in other states, open support of a candidate by organized labor can be damaging.

Though a large share of labor's money goes to Democratic candidates, most union leaders speak of labor as an independent political force. They follow a policy of nonpartisan endorsement and put strong restrictions on the use of resources given to Democratic party leaders.

However, in parts of New York, New Jersey, Pennsylvania, California, Illinois, and Ohio, labor has taken over some of the functions of the Democratic party. In Michigan, competing factions of labor have fought for control of the Democratic party.

Three main channels of labor's activity in politics are visible. In congressional districts, cities, counties, and communities, it operates through trade unions and their locals. At state and national levels, it works through a loose confederation of AFL and CIO regional groups. Overall, and often reaching down into cities and counties, there is the operation of COPE and its action groups.

Four kinds of political money feed through these channels into campaigns:

• Individual contributions. One of every eight union members contributes to campaigns. Because of labor's interest in campaigns and the efforts of union leaders to educate their members, almost a third of those who make small contributions to politicians belong to labor-union families.

• Contributions from union treasuries. This dues money may be used in most states for candidates running for non-federal offices.

• Educational expenses. Funds from dues produce the materials that inform union members about candidates and issues and urge them to register and vote.

• Public service activities, such as sponsoring news programs. These are also paid for by dues money and may have a definite union slant.

As in the case of business and wealthy individuals, there is no way of determining how many millions are spent in each election campaign by labor unions. Most of the money goes into campaigns at state and national levels through special committees. Some is transferred to political action groups. A few unions, such as the United Mine Workers and the Teamsters, have taken the position that their spending was done at the local level and was not subject to requirements to report it to the House of Representatives.

The number of small, individual contributors, estimated at several million, is increasing steadily, though slowly. In many cases, volunteer services and gifts of goods play a larger part than contributions of money. Campaign workers get paint and materials from a local store to fix up a candidate's headquarters. Young people put up street banners. Supporters make their own signs and set them in front yards on main streets. All these things help to trim down the power of the big contributors.

Still, the fact remains: one-third of the contributors provide two-thirds of the money which goes into campaigns.

To keep the two-party system alive and, hopefully, to make certain that they are taken care of no matter which party wins, some businessmen give equal sums to both sides. In this group are aircraft manufacturers; the owners of buslines; textile manufacturers; brewers; makers of automobiles, watches, tires, and doughnuts; airline executives; retailers; and bankers.

Law firms are another source of party funds. Frequently, they serve as the agents of wealthy people to funnel money into the coffers of both parties, often to candidates with sharply conflicting views. It is only when these candidates happen to run against each other that an embarrassing situation can develop.

No one knows all the intricate arrangements used to get money into a campaign. In many cases, it passes through several hands before reaching the committee that will use it.

Big donors show up on the lists of both parties. Most of the officers and directors of the nation's biggest corporations make substantial contributions to one party or the other. At the top levels, they are largely slanted toward the Republicans. Dr. Alexander Heard in a study of campaign giving by the top executives of 350 of the nation's richest corporations found that fewer than 4 percent gave their money to the Democrats. Down the line, among medium-sized and smaller industries, Dr. Heard found a great many contributors to Democrats.

In a hot campaign, corporation employees often are prodded by letters from top company executives into giving to one party or another. This pressure can be highly effective. In a recent election contest, an important official of a major automobile firm was on the finance committee of his party. The firm allowed him to call together a group of company dealers and solicit them for funds for the party. The dealers were asked to spread the word to other automobile people whom they knew personally. The pressure was enough to produce action. Dealers said they felt this was the voice of the company and they gave money. They said that if the pressure had been put on them to give to the opposite party, they would have sent their money in the other direction. They did not give as partisans.

Where the law permits corporations to spend money in state campaigns, some do, as they have in California, Indiana, New Jersey, and Wisconsin. There have been occasions when corporations and labor have collided in campaigns in which right-to-work laws were at stake.

Students of campaign spending report that many legal prohibitions are ignored by all concerned. Contributions from labor unions and from corporate treasuries manage to get into campaigns despite the laws. A ban against buying goods, advertising, and performing other services for federal candidates sometimes is forgotten. A law against accepting contributions from those holding U.S. government contracts goes unheeded. Limits on the amount any one person may give to a candidate are dodged by using other names and spreading the money among several committees. The law says that a candidate must not promise appointment to any federal or private job. Yet, big campaign contributors regularly wind up in plush jobs when their man wins. The promises, implied or real, have been made by campaign managers, not by the candidates.

Forty-three states require some sort of report covering campaign spending. Seven—Alaska, Delaware, Georgia, Illinois, Louisiana, Nebraska, and Rhode Island—make no attempt to regulate spending. Of the forty-three that do make such an effort, only ten call for detailed reports from the candidates and their committees, telling where the money comes from and how it was spent, before both the primaries and the general election.

There are wide variations in the state laws. In several states that require reports, the average voter has virtually no way of knowing who is paying for the campaign of any candidate. In Tennessee, statements of expense for statewide primaries—which often decide who is to be the elected official—are filed with the chairman of the party's executive committee, not with a state official. These reports are not available to the public. In Michigan, reports are filed in the counties; anyone wishing to know about statewide spending must track down the figures county by county. In Indiana, the reports for statewide committees may be filed in the county of residence of the committee treasurer. For this reason, the treasurers often are chosen from some out-of-the-way county.

Many states make a real effort to let the people know who is paying the costs for their officeholders. Montana and Oregon require that the actual ledgers and account books be brought in for inspection by a representative of the opposing candidate or his treasurer. Maine and Oregon publish for general distribution a summary of spending in both the primary and the general election. In a few states, such as Texas, state officials are not permitted to require state employees to pay a "political assessment." In other states, this is a common practice. In Arkansas, there is a ban against hauling voters to the polls in a primary election. In several other states, such as Michigan and Utah, only the sick, disabled, or infirm may be given transportation to the polls.

What many authorities regard as a model law was enacted in Florida in 1951. It permits unlimited spending but requires that all spending and contributions, including services as well as cash, be made public. No more than $1,000 may be given by any one person. Those with permits for dog or horse racing are forbidden to contribute. So are those who operate a public utility or who have liquor licenses. Some candidates are required to make financial reports on a weekly basis.

In the same year that Florida enacted this law, North Carolina erased its limitation on the amount that could be spent in a campaign. Three years later, nine important politicians in the state were asked how the change had affected spending. They replied that they could see no difference.

In an earlier day—before such things as Corrupt Practices Laws were invented—Senator Boies Penrose, then boss of Pennsylvania politics, once told a friend:

> Last week one of our statesmen who comes from the noble west came to me with tears in his voice. Seems he'd been devoting too much of his time to noble-mindedness. He had read all about England, France, Russia, Japan and Germany and was telling the country all about it, while he should have been doing something for the railroads out his way. . . . They elected him— the railroads—and if you hire out to a man he has the right to expect something.
>
> Well, they had told him that as a Senator he was about through, that, as long as he had gone in for this stateman business, they'd have to look further for a hired man. Took all the wind out of our statesman. . . . What was the use being a statesman if you hadn't any job to practice it in. Back home he's just a country lawyer. Six thousand dollars a year. . . .
>
> Finally I made them listen to reason. I had to tell them that I'd be responsible for their senator after this—for their statesman. I had to give them my word that he'd shut up and go to work and stop talking about Europe and Asia. So, when he came around to me next day with more tears, I told him it was all right, that he'd be reelected. So we're shy one stateman now.[1]

We have come a long way since that day, but we have yet a long way to go before ensuring an equal opportunity for candidates through an equal distribution of funds and communications facilities.

---

[1] Davenport, Walter. *Power and Glory: The Life of Boies Penrose.* New York: G. P. Putnam's Sons, 1931. pp. 189-90.

PART 2

CHAPTER SEVEN / **First Rung: The Local Level**

Government starts at the door of the citizen: the front door when children leave for school; the back door when garbage and trash collectors call.

Politics is just as close. In a well-organized community, it begins when a party worker pays a visit or sends literature; in a rural area, when a candidate or a neighbor asks a person to vote in a particular way. From the voting precinct it reaches upward to the town, city, or county. Most politicians embark upon their careers with party work or election to offices in the home community.

Many things that reach into our daily lives are handled at the local level. The fire department and the local ambulance respond to emergency calls. The policeman and sheriff are charged with keeping order. The county clerk handles wills and records deeds. County and city officials choose teachers for schools and decide what is to be built next or where a new road is to be located.

Counties, cities, towns and the wide variety of special districts that operate on the local scene are created by states through their legislatures. They are an arm of state government in the area. Each branch of local government is set up through special legislation that spells out in detail the boundaries of the area subject to its control, the degree of control to be exercised by the local agency, and the duties and powers of the officials of the agency.

There is no accurate figure for the number of officials in city and county governments in the United States. The latest tabulation of the International City Managers' Association shows that there are 3,043 counties, 18,000 municipalities, 18,000 special districts, 17,000 townships, 35,000 school districts, and 2,000 additional school systems operating under different arrangements. The number of elected officials for these separate units of local government varies from city to city, town to town, and county to county within each state, according to the whims or needs of the communities involved.

The amount of money flowing through these agencies into the communities is anybody's guess. It runs into many billions of dollars and is an admixture of local, state, and federal funds. The payroll for local governmental units is about $3 billion a month.

There are organized county governments in all states except Alaska, Connecticut, and Rhode Island. Texas has the largest number of counties with 254; Delaware has the fewest with 3. San Bernardino in California is the largest county. It contains 20,000 square miles and could hold 20 states the size of Rhode Island, or 10 as large as Delaware, or 2 Vermonts or Marylands or Massachusettses with room left over for a few extra counties.

In forty-nine states, the word for this unit of government is county; in Louisiana, it is called a parish because of the state's French and Spanish heritage. The number of counties in all states changes from time to time. In 1962, Connecticut wiped out its eight counties. But in the same year, Wisconsin created a new one.

Most students of government agree that two-thirds of the counties could be abolished by rearranging boundaries and combining facilities. Thousands of officeholders could be taken off the public payrolls. Local government would be more efficient and there would be a subsequent saving in tax money. Franklin D. Roosevelt proposed such a change in the 1930s but without success. Most of the present counties were created in the horse and buggy days so that a man could drive comfortably from his home to the county seat and return in one day.

Fewer than 350 of the 3,043 counties contain 100,000 people. Five counties in California, Colorado, Hawaii, and Texas have fewer than 500 residents. A dozen others in Colorado, Idaho, Montana, Nebraska, Nevada, and Texas have fewer than 1,000. Five of these counties are larger than the state of Rhode Island; one is twice as large.

The average county has between 10,000 and 25,000 citizens, maintaining a full staff of officials. Some of these are so poorly paid that they practice law from offices in the courthouse, or let a relative handle county affairs while they earn a livelihood elsewhere.

Relations between cities and counties are mixed. In eleven cities, such as New York, Philadelphia, and New Orleans, certain county offices are merged with those of the cities. Denver, Honolulu, and San Francisco are designated as city-county units and operate primarily as cities. Thirty-six cities operate outside any county area and handle all the functions usually performed by counties. Thirty-three of these are in Virginia. The others are Baltimore, St. Louis, and the District of Columbia.

The abolition of county government in Connecticut has not worked as well as politicians had expected. They now wonder whether it would have been better to abolish some of the city and township governments instead to get a better coordination of functions.

An example of this alternative can be found in Maryland. Silver Spring, one of the largest cities in the state, has no city government, no city officials, no city taxes, no city school system, no city police. All services are provided by Montgomery County, thus eliminating one layer of taxes for the citizens.

The governmental structure can become confusing when counties get involved with big cities. New York state is more confusing than most. The complications are such that even the people who live there have trouble understanding them. Fifty-seven of the counties are divided into cities and towns. Two or more towns may be incorporated in one village, but a village may also extend over two or more township lines.

Nassau County, for instance, has 3 towns and 2 cities. Inside the towns are 64 incorporated villages. The county also has 269 special districts and 57 school districts. All of these areas of government are manned by officials, many with overlapping responsibilities.

New York City is composed of five counties with limited powers. Outside New York City—in fifty-seven counties of the state—business is conducted by boards composed of supervisors of the towns and cities in the county. Each county elects a sheriff, district attorney, county clerk, county treasurer, and a few other officials.

Illinois has three kinds of counties. Some are organized on a township basis, some are not. Township counties have boards of supervisors plus at least twelve other elected officials. All counties have a governing board. Finally, there is Cook County, which is so entangled with the city of Chicago that few can tell where one leaves off and the other begins.

In California, 90 percent of the people live in 10 metropolitan areas. The state has 58 counties, 400 cities, and 3,000 special districts, all vastly complicated. The counties exercise administrative functions, collect taxes, and build roads. But most of their power has been sapped away by the special districts.

Each of the seventy-one counties in Wisconsin has a county board consisting of the chairmen of town boards, a supervisor for each ward in cities, and a supervisor for each village in the county. This adds up to some 2,600 county supervisors. In addition, each county elects a sheriff, coroner, recorder of deeds, and district attorney.

More than half of the population of Texas lives in 18 of the 254 counties. But each county in the state has about the same governmental structure. There also are 15 metropolitan areas. Sometimes six or seven different police groups will operate in a metropolitan county. There is a vast overlapping of authority in taxing, police and fire protection, water supply, airports, and health.

Each Texas county elects a county judge and four county commissioners, a county clerk, county attorney, sheriff, tax collector-assessor, four justices of the peace, and constables. Counties with more than 10,000 population add to these a treasurer and surveyor, a public weigher, and an inspector of hides and animals.

Salaries in large counties can be high. A study by the National Association of Counties found that top officials in counties with populations between 100,000 and 250,000 peaked at around $23,000 a year. Important officials in counties with 250,000 to 500,000 population could earn $30,000, while counties with 500,000 to 750,000 paid up to $35,000. Here, they leveled off. Above 750,000 in population, cities tended to take over the most important functions and paid the highest salaries.

In some states, there are lively contests for local offices. But much of rural America shows little interest in these offices. Even in big suburban counties, the candidates seeking these offices usually are only a name to the voter.

A study by Thomas Kitsos at the University of Illinois in 1966 showed that more than half of those elected to county offices in that state had no real opposition in the elections of that year. These included county clerks, sheriffs, treasurers, and superintendents of schools. The study covered both primaries and general elections.

One study of rural counties in Iowa found that in more than a third of the state there was no competition for any county office either in the primary or the general election. More than half of the counties had no contest for any office in the primaries.

Many refuse office in the government of the average rural county because of the small pay and minor authority. In one western state, county offices were regarded as so unattractive that no capable person in either party wanted to run. There was trouble finding candidates for county commissioner, state legislator, county clerk, or clerk of the court. At a party meeting, it was necessary to draft candidates for these offices to round out the ticket, even though there was no doubt that the men on the ticket would be elected.

Except in big counties or cities where the stakes are higher and the glory shines brighter, studies show that the average courthouse crowd stays in office year after year, election after election. County courthouse officials with their families and hangers-on comprise the heart of local political organizations. In many states, this is the party machine. These people control the choice of candidates for the state legislature, and this tends to put them in a privileged category. The officials do little favors for friends and carry on the small affairs of the county and stay in office. Only a scandal or the appearance of a man with driving political ambition can shake them loose. Even a presidential sweep by the opposition party often leaves county officials unscathed.

County elections in Illinois, according to Kitsos's study, indicated that primaries were held simply to ratify decisions made elsewhere. This pointed to a weakness often found in county systems, both rural and urban.

In rural counties, decisions about the top candidates—sheriff, county judge, county commissioners—usually are determined by a small group whose interests are affected by actions of the county government. They own large tracts of land. They run banks and can call the shot for loans. They run automobile agencies. They hold liquor licenses. They build county roads. Either in person or through their spokesmen, they arrive at an informal decision about the candidates.

This decision is passed along to dominant party people in the county. It often happens that one or more of the interested parties is already chairman or a member of the party committee.

Now and then, a local politician gets completely out of hand, makes an issue of "bossism," develops his own following among the electorate, and takes off on a course of his own. He makes a name for himself by fighting the "interests." Sometimes, there is a scandal as the rebel undertakes an investigation and puts his evidence before a grand jury. Often, the rebel is induced to run for higher office. The county rulers move him off to Congress or into the state government to get him out of local affairs. Many a high-level politician started this way. He was eased out of county and local government into the state legislature, from which he leaped into state or national politics.

Usually at the local level, two groups are scrambling for control. The big landowner, the banker, the automobile dealer, the liquor distributor, the contractor—all have a competitor eager for his own share of county favors. The opposition group hacks away at the alliance that has control and works out an arrangement of its own until it can come up with candidates and issues with which it can hope to win. When this happens, there is a real struggle for the top spots in the county. It may be inside the dominant party in a primary. It can come from the opposition party in the general election.

While a few telephone calls or casual conversations often can decide the outcome in a rural county, the process is more complicated in a big county. This may contain a small city or it may be a big suburban complex on the outskirts of a large city.

In such a county, pressure groups arise to make it more difficult for political handlers. The suburban counties fall into turmoil every two to four years, depending on how often officials are elected. Teacher organizations get into the act with demands for bigger salaries and smaller classes. Citizens' groups demand to be heard; often they form countywide alliances that are a potential threat to the ruling political groups.

Union labor takes a hand in industrial counties. It develops action groups in shops, factories, and offices. These are responsible for making every union member familiar with the record of officials from his precinct and election district. Union leaders are recruited to get people to the polls in their own districts. In the interplay of these forces, a larger degree of democracy makes itself felt.

If the county is large and the process of getting elected is more difficult, the prizes are bigger for the money-men who put up most of the campaign funds. Large landowners want zoning permits. Builders seek favors from county inspectors. There is more money for the bankers to handle. More automobiles are needed for county services. More roads and streets are to be built. Fire, health, and building inspectors can make things rough for a businessman. Tax assessments can be tampered with. People grow rich from being appointed as receivers and guardians.

Politics in a big county or city takes on the appearance of state and national campaigns. There is the pattern of negotiation and alliance with strong groups and dominant personalities.

After election, the winning candidate is expected to remember his friends. This adds to the enthusiasm that local candidates put into the effort to elect the rest of his ticket. Local candidates and county leaders are convinced that those communities carried by a candidate for governor or senator will get more attention from the top people when it comes to choosing locations for new highways, vocational schools, junior colleges, and other state and federal institutions.

For the local party leaders, there is also the hope that their work in getting votes will be remembered by state party directors when there is a good job to be filled or a top spot open in the party. Few counties have a merit system for hiring employees, a point that helps to elicit campaign work from those who have jobs and want to keep them, or those who seek a job.

Voters increasingly are demanding candidates of integrity with an understanding of public affairs. There is a trend away from partisan politics.

Many cities and counties are employing professional managers. Policies are set by city and county councils whose members are elected on a nonpartisan basis. Most party politicians oppose such systems. They leave less room for political manipulation, fewer jobs and contracts with which to reward the faithful, less leeway to swing favors for those who pay for campaigns.

Quite a few cities have turned to the nonpartisan election of mayors. Where they have not, social reforms and civil service systems have so warn down the power of parties that few of the old city machines are left. Instead of bread and coal distributed long ago by precinct captains, people in need get welfare and social security checks. The smart politicians of today are those who teach the needy in their areas to take advantage of the many facilities available to them.

The office of mayor is increasing steadily in importance. The mayor must deal with riots, crime, and slum clearance. He must handle federal programs to rejuvenate the cities and make them habitable. The old picture of the playboy mayor produced by machine politics is fading away.

The mayor has moved into the center of things. He has more personal contact with the federal government than the governor. Many federal programs bypass the statehouse and feed directly into the cities. The mayor of a Pacific coast city reports that for every one trip to his state capital, he makes ten to Washington. The mayor of Atlanta called the problems of the cities totally foreign to state government and said that the major thrust in solving them must come from the federal government.

Big-city mayors confer with federal and state officials about programs for their community. They have a chance to dicker and negotiate. But in smaller towns, the problems and programs move too fast for novices. The home-grown politician, thrust up by local politicking is out of his depth. As things grow more complex, elected officials in small cities sometimes get ignored.

The case of a town in Arizona, population 9,000, provides an example. It was a sleepy cotton growers' community, not far from an Indian reservation. Then government money and services began streaming into the town.

Money flowed into the schools, some of it for teaching Indian children. There were free lunches, milk programs, summer fellowships for teachers, new books on farming. Equipment was provided for vocational training: a truck, radios, tools, stoves. dishwashers, and a link trainer for future pilots.

A clinic offered treatment for tuberculosis and venereal diseases. Nurses helped with maternal and child care. Polio vaccine was administered. A county health building sprang up, and study of mental health was undertaken.

The economy got a lift. There were soil payments, guaranteed cotton prices, grants, and loans for soil conservation. Programs were developed to brighten homes and enliven the community: homemakers' clubs, 4-H clubs for young people, technical meetings. There were inspections for industrial safety, samplings to test the purity of food and drugs, examinations to protect bank deposits, mail delivery, and the draft board.

The outside world had moved in on the small town. The bulk of the welfare payments which 3 percent of the townspeople received came from federal and state funds. Social security and money for new health facilities and the town's community hospital came from federal agencies. A local office of the state employment commission was financed by both the state and the federal government.

The main street was a highway paved by the state and the federal government. The chief of police was trained by the Federal Bureau of Investigation and used its laboratory facilities when needed. The jail, which sometimes held federal prisoners, was built with advice from the United States Bureau of Prisons. Federal grants took care of the first city planning. The sewer system, the airport, a mountain park, twenty low-cost housing units, and the National Guard Armory all went into place with help from the federal government.

It was as if Washington and Phoenix had taken over the town. Locally elected officials simply watched the money go by.

Across the nation, population shifts are having their own impact on politics. The influx of Negroes from southern farms to cities and the outflow of whites into the suburbs are changing both the complexion and the voting characteristics of cities.

Negro votes now are a decisive factor in elections in more than a dozen cities. In many cases, these votes are important enough to determine the direction electoral votes of a state will go. Among the major cities involved in this trend are New York, Philadelphia, Los Angeles, San Francisco, Chicago, Cleveland, Cincinnati, Detroit, St. Louis, Atlanta, Memphis, Nashville, Louisville, and Baltimore.

Cleveland was the first of the big cities to elect a Negro mayor. He was Carl B. Stokes, who was born in a poor neighborhood of that city and came up the hard way. His father died when he was two. His mother brought up two children on her wages as a cleaning woman, helped for a time by welfare money. The boys delivered newspapers and worked in neighborhood stores. The mother kept insisting: "If you study hard, you've got to become somebody."

Young Stokes was a high school dropout. He worked for a while in a foundry and signed up for the army at eighteen. After World War II, he went back to high school and worked his way through college as a law enforcement agent and as a waiter on a dining car. He earned a law degree, became a probation officer for the municipal court, then assistant prosecutor, and finally a member of the legislature. On his second try, he won election as mayor of Cleveland.

The first large southern city to elect a Negro in the upper

brackets of government was Atlanta. It chose Maynard Holbrook Jackson as vice mayor. He defeated a highly respected businessman, William Farris, who had served for sixteen years on the Board of Aldermen. Mr. Farris did not raise the race issue in his campaign. Mr. Jackson got about a third of the white votes and 90 percent of those from Negroes.

The election of Mr. Jackson as vice mayor and Sam Massell as mayor cracked a coalition of wealth which had dominated politics in that city for thirty years. Some point to this election as a sign of great changes taking place in American politics.

CHAPTER EIGHT / Up the Ladder: The State Level

The man who makes it to the governor's chair is about as far up the ladder as most politicians can expect to go. He is one of the fifty top state executives in the nation. In most cases, he is also leader of his party in the state. He has many jobs at his disposal and exercises great influence. He can help his friends and injure his enemies.

Under most state constitutions, the governor holds command of armed forces and is the chief law enforcement officer. As chief of his party, he has an important role in shaping legislation. He can veto measures passed by the legislature.

Those who helped him into the governor's chair have no absolute power to compel him to do anything. Yet, in many cases, the newly elected governor finds himself bound by implied, if not specified, promises or commitments to those who put up the money to pay for his election costs.

The governor is the directing head of the most basic structure in American government. The states were here long before there was a federal government. In the main, the pattern for state government was set by Great Britain in the colonies before the American Revolution. After the Revolution, each state became a free-wheeling entity and remained as such under the

111

Confederation of States. Each state guarded its rights and powers so jealously that the Confederation became a helpless and totally frustrated agency. Bitter quarrels over the rights of citizens in one state to engage in commerce across state lines with the citizens of other states, plus an outright rebellion in Massachusetts, finally convinced a group of important leaders that they must create a strong national government, even at the expense of giving up some state powers.

Out of this conviction came the Constitutional Convention and the careful diplomatic negotiations among the states that persuaded them to yield enough of their own powers to establish a federal government. In exchange for the powers granted to the federal government, each state was guaranteed a republican form of government, protection against foreign invasion and domestic insurrection, and that the citizen of each state would have the same rights and privileges guaranteed to all citizens of the United States. Each state promised to respect the supremacy of the Constitution and the laws and treaties of the United States.

The states still hold strong powers to regulate the daily affairs of their own people. They establish and maintain organized government at state and local levels. They regulate voting, subject to the condition that no citizen may be deprived of the right to vote because of race or color. They levy taxes. They make and enforce laws to maintain the peace, protect public health and morals, and promote the common welfare, subject to the limitation that no person may be deprived of life, liberty or property without due process of law. Each has wide powers in education and the provision of public services, and can create corporations and handle the whole range of private laws that regulate institutions, families and the handling of private property within their borders.

The governors of the fifty states direct the spending of a total of about $60 billion a year. Much of this goes for schools and colleges, public welfare, and hospitals. Some of it goes for highways and other kinds of construction as well as for purchases of supplies for state institutions. About an eighth of the

How Our Two Major Parties Nominate Candidates in Each State

State	By Primary	By Convention	State	By Primary	By Convention
Ala.	Dem	Rep	Mont.	Rep—Dem	
Alaska	Rep—Dem		Nebr.	Rep—Dem	
Ariz.	Rep—Dem		Nev.	Rep—Dem	
Ark.	Rep—Dem		N.H.	Rep—Dem	
Calif.	Rep—Dem		N.J.	Rep—Dem	
Colo.	Rep—Dem	Rep—Dem[1]	N. Mex.	Rep—Dem	
Conn.		Rep—Dem[2]	N.Y.	Rep—Dem	Rep—Dem[4]
Del.		Rep—Dem[2]	N.C.	Rep—Dem	
Fla.	Rep—Dem		N. Dak.	Rep—Dem	Rep—Dem[5]
Ga.	Rep—Dem		Ohio	Rep—Dem	
Hawaii	Rep—Dem		Okla.	Rep—Dem	
Idaho		Rep—Dem[2]	Oreg.	Rep—Dem	
Ill.	Rep—Dem		Pa.	Rep—Dem	
Ind.	Rep—Dem[3]	Rep—Dem[3]	R.I.	Rep—Dem	Rep—Dem[6]
Iowa	Rep—Dem		S.C.	Rep—Dem	Rep—Dem
Kans.	Rep—Dem		S. Dak.	Rep—Dem	
Ky.	Rep—Dem		Tenn.	Rep—Dem	
La.	Rep—Dem		Texas	Rep—Dem	
Maine	Rep—Dem		Utah	Rep—Dem	Rep—Dem[7]
Md.	Rep—Dem		Vt.	Rep—Dem	
Mass.	Rep—Dem		Va.	Dem	Rep
Mich.	Rep—Dem		Wash.	Dem	
Minn.	Rep—Dem		W. Va.	Rep—Dem	
Miss.	Rep—Dem		Wis.	Rep—Dem	Rep[8]
Mo.	Rep—Dem		Wyo.	Rep—Dem	

[1] Party conventions may designate one or more candidates, who receive priority position on primary ballot. Actual nomination is in the primary.

[2] Nominations are made by party conventions. Any unsuccessful candidate for a nomination who receives at least 20 percent (35 percent in Delaware) of the convention vote may, if he wishes, require the nomination to be settled at a primary election.

[3] Senate candidates are chosen by party conventions; House candidates are selected in the primary.

[4] Nomination for statewide office is made by state party committees. Any candidate receiving at least 25 percent of the state committee vote may require the nomination to be settled at a primary election.

[5] Party conventions only endorse candidates; nomination is in the primary.

[6] State committees only endorse candidates; nomination is in the primary.

[7] State conventions designate names for ballot. If candidate receives more than 80 percent of the convention vote, he is nominated. Otherwise the top two contenders in convention balloting are certified for the primary election.

[8] Republicans endorse statewide candidates in convention; actual nomination is in the primary. U.S. House candidates are endorsed in district caucuses.

Source: U.S. Senate Library

total amount handled by the states comes from the federal government.

In order to protect the governor—and the state—from his friends, many states have created commissions to handle a great deal of the money and some of the major policies. A governor may appoint his friends to these commissions as the terms of commissioners expire, but usually it is not possible for him in one term of office to pack the commissions with enough friends to dictate decisions. For this reason, some states allow a governor only one term of office. After that, he must skip at least one term.

The pay scale for governors ranges from $10,000 a year in Arkansas and North Dakota to $50,000 in New York. Most earn about $20,000 a year. Few if any could hope to win office with advances equal only to the governor's total salary for either the two- or four-year term to which they are elected.

A campaign for governor brings both large sums of money and a massive movement of people into the fray. Hundreds of offices, involving control of the statehouse, the two houses of the legislature, and county officials all down the line, are at stake in such a campaign. Far more jobs are available to winning politicians at the state level than at the federal level. A governor alone can make hundreds, sometimes thousands, of appointments. U.S. senators and representatives have little with which to reward party workers. In almost every state, members of a party would rather lose all of their seats in Congress than a governorship. Each of the 100 parties lives on the jobs it can win at the state and local levels. The monthly payroll for all state employees runs to about $1 billion, or an average of about $20 million for each state.

To become governor, a candidate first must make himself known to and trusted by the county leaders of his party. He must put together a personal following among people who know how to raise campaign funds. He must enlist the support of people who will fight for his nomination in a state convention or in a primary campaign. This means that he must meet with top party leaders, fund-raisers, and spokesmen for various factions in big counties around the state.

Once a man has been chosen by his party as its candidate for governor, he must try to unite all factions that opposed his nomination. He becomes the leader of a ticket including half a dozen or more candidates for statewide offices, most of the aspirants to the state legislature, and all candidates for county and local offices. This can give him an army of thousands of workers: the candidates, members of their families, local party workers across the state, and their friends. Money for the campaign then flows in from hundreds of sources all along the line.

In the Northeast, where two-party campaigns have been a fact of political life throughout most of American history, fund-raising practices and alliances with moneyed people are taken for granted. They are becoming more important in the South, where Democrats suddenly are being confronted with the costs of a two-party system and the need for full-fledged state organizations. In the past, Democrats had little to fear from Republicans. Now, with both Republicans and television costs to reckon with, Southern Democrats are alarmed. Republicans usually avoid expensive primaries in the South by naming their candidates in conventions. But Democrats have to fight for a place on the party ticket.

Tom Adams, a secretary of state for Florida, pulled out of a race for the governorship and quit politics, providing an insight into the conditions under which a candidate for governor may have to run. He explained that to raise money for his campaign he would have had to make so many promises to those seeking favors that his hands would have been tied as governor. Mr. Adams listed some of the interests involved: road contractors; industries that pollute the air and water and do not want to be put to the expense of installing controls; suppliers of automobiles and equipment to the state; land developers; industries demanding tax concessions; applicants for state licenses; engineers, architects, and other professional people seeking state business.

The costs of a few recent campaigns tend to support Mr.

Adams's statement. In 1966, Haydon Burns spent $1.6 million in a race for the Democratic nomination to be governor of Florida—and lost. In North Carolina, estimates of the price for running in a general election for governor have risen to $1 million for each candidate. Even with the backing of her husband's strong state organization, cost estimates of the race of Mrs. Lurleen Wallace for governor of Alabama run to $500,000. In Tennessee and Mississippi, no candidate reports spending more than $25,000 because that is the top limit allowed. Yet cost estimates for campaigns in those states run from $250,000 up.

An exception to the mounting costs of successful campaigning may be found in Georgia. There, Lester Maddox, caught up in a tide of segregationist emotion, spent only about $40,000 to win election as governor. However, it cost Ellis Arnall more than a million dollars to lose the Democratic nomination and Howard H. Callaway, a Republican, about the same amount to lose in the general election that year. The Georgia legislature repealed a law requiring reports of campaign expenses because it turned out to be ineffective.

Students of politics report that as campaign expenses rise, the power of the back-room managers grows. In general, it is said, those who provide campaign money in the South are those who demand that taxes on business be kept low and that labor union activities be held to a minimum in order to attract more industries. Most of the big money comes from executives of banks, railroad companies, public utilities, insurance companies, trucking lines, and loan companies. In a changing economy, however, more and more union labor money is being fed into southern campaigns—as elsewhere.

In most states, the final choice of a party's candidates for the various state offices is left to the voters in primary elections. However, the choice usually amounts to confirming the candidate picked by the party leaders and financial backers. The outcome of a primary election is in the hands of those who take the trouble to vote. Voter turnout for primaries often falls to about a third of those eligible to take part. Those who vote are most likely to follow the wishes of party leaders. It is only occasionally that a strong personality emerges with enough financial backing to buck the party organization.

The right to vote in a primary election usually is restricted to those who are registered as members of the party holding the primary. This means that those registered as independents have no voice in choosing the candidates of the two major parties. Similarly, those registered as members of any minority party, such as George Wallace's Independent party, may not vote in the primary of a major party in most states.

A few states, such as Wisconsin, permit registered voters to cast their ballots in the primary of either party. This means that Republicans can cross over to vote in Democratic primaries, either because they like a particular candidate or because they think he will be easier game for a Republican opponent to defeat in the general election. In such states, Democrats will, of course, vote in Republican primaries for the same reasons. Quite a few states, particularly in the South, require no party designation by the voter when he registers. This leaves the registrant free to vote in the primary of the dominant party if he wishes.

In most states, prospective candidates can get their names on the ballot for a primary election simply by declaring themselves and paying a filing fee. In some cases, they are required to get a specific number of signatures on a petition. State laws specify how many signatures are needed and who is qualified to sign. Usually any qualified voter may sign.

Primary elections are held from March in New Hampshire to October in Hawaii. The big season for primary elections is in even-numbered years, when most officials are elected.

Usually, a party's nomination goes to the candidate getting the largest number of votes. However, eleven southern and border states, where Democrats have been dominant for 100 years, require a candidate to get a majority of the votes in a primary to win the nomination. If a contender fails to get a majority, the two candidates with the largest number of votes run against each other in a second primary. This has the effect of creating two parties, each built around a personality.

Primary campaigns are conducted in the same manner as those for a general election. Candidates do all they can to get their own supporters to the polls. The one who enjoys open support of the party organization has a great advantage.

Direct choice of candidates by voters in a primary election was first employed by Crawford County, Pennsylvania, in the 1860s. Various localities began to adopt the plan during the remaining years of the nineteenth century, and the system gained impetus in the early 1900s. Wisconsin was the first state to put the primary into use for the choice of statewide candidates. It now is employed by every state in one form or another.

In 1903, as the drive for statewide use of the primary system was gaining force, Professor James Albert Woodburn of Indiana University wrote:

> If the people are to rule under party government, the party organization and its action must be brought under popular control; party government must be made truly representative in order that the majority may rule. The fundamental purpose of primary election reform is to secure this by taking party elections, preliminary to the general election, out of unregulated, irresponsible private management and by placing those elections under regulated State control, with provision against fraud, mistake, or neglect, where every man may count one, and no man more than one, where there will be equal chances for all and special chances for none. If the party is to be regarded as a kind of private corporation whose business is to be managed by a set of professionals; and if in the party primary, or caucus, the boss is to appoint the chairman who is to name the committee to name the delegates; if party caucuses are called to meet in saloons or other uncomfortable or disreputable places; and if the professional chairman makes decisions according to the "majority of noise," or appoints counters to count the votes that

have been deposited in a hat passed around in a promis-
cuous crowd; or if, after delegates are elected at precinct
meetings, the convention through its "credentials committee" in star chamber, always finds, or makes, a majority
subservient to the boss,—then no matter how much honest
men may strive in the party they will find striving in vain.
They will quit politics as unprofitable business. They will
retire from party meetings and the party will be given
over more and more to the unscrupulous professionals.
This is what has happened to a large extent.

The convention method of nominating candidates still is
used in several states where party control is fairly strong. Party
leaders do not want the nominating process to get out of hand.
In such states, the party machinery reaches down to the county
or precinct level. Local leaders usually can be depended on to
produce delegates for conventions who will support the candidate preferred by the party's dominant group.

Use of the convention process varies, and laws are changed
from time to time to suit the political needs of the party in
power.

In Indiana and Delaware, candidates for statewide offices
—governor, senator, and statehouse officials—are nominated in
convention. This puts the selection process beyond the reach
of the average voter. Delegates to state conventions are picked
at local and county meetings attended in most cases by a collection of party workers.

Connecticut for years has used conventions to pick candidates for different government offices. State conventions choose
candidates for governor and statewide offices. Congressional
district conventions pick candidates for the House of Representatives. Town and city committees select candidates for
local areas. But at each level, the losing contender for party
nomination can force a primary election to test the sentiment

---

[1] Woodburn, James Albert. *Political Parties and Party Problems in the
United States.* New York: G. P. Putnam's Sons, 1903. pp. 284-85.

of voters if he gets a required percentage of delegate votes in convention.

Variations of these methods are used in Colorado, Idaho, Massachusetts, Nebraska, Rhode Island, and Utah. In Colorado, candidates who get 20 percent of the votes in convention go into a primary contest. In Utah, the convention designates two candidates who fight it out in a primary. Rhode Island and Idaho use a similar system, but candidates who wish to challenge the decision of the convention might get on the ballot through petition.

Few voters in a legislative district have any knowledge of the candidates for whom they are voting. Yet members of state legislatures are more important than voters generally realize.

The legislative branch has powers on a par with those of the governor. It fixes the rules regulating the activities of individuals and businesses inside state boundaries. It sets the tax rates and the rules for state administrative agencies. It carves out the boundaries of jurisdiction for cities and counties. It decides how state money is to be apportioned among various agencies.

Legislatures in every state except one are patterned after the U.S. Congress. Nebraska has a one-house, or unicameral, legislature, which performs the same duties as do the two houses in other states.

Each house of the forty-nine other legislatures is of equal status. Under state constitutions, as under the federal constitution, there is no upper or lower house, and such qualitative references, while applicable to European parliaments, are inaccurate in the case of U.S. legislative institutions.

The state senate is smaller numerically than the other branch of the legislature, and each member represents a larger geographic area and more people than does a member of the other house. There are almost 2,000 members of the Senate in the forty-nine bicameral state legislatures, as compared with 6,700 in the other chamber. State senators are elected for four-year terms in thirty-six states and for two-

New trends. (Above) For the first time since Reconstruction days, a Republican wins the governorship of Virginia. Linwood Holton, the new Governor, is seen above with President Nixon. (Below) The rising influence of the Negro vote is reflected in the election of Carl B. Stokes, seen being sworn in as the first Negro mayor of Cleveland.

year terms in thirteen states.

While all states agree on calling one chamber the Senate, only forty-one refer to the other as the House of Representatives. In Maryland, Virginia, and West Virginia, it is called a House of Delegates. In California, Nevada, New Jersey, New York, and Wisconsin, it is called the Assembly or the General Assembly. Members of this branch serve two-year terms in all states except Alabama, Louisiana, Maryland, and Mississippi, where they are elected for four-year terms.

Pay is the same for members of both houses in the forty-nine states that have them. The pay scale tends to reflect the size of the population in the state. Of the seventeen states that pay more than $10,000 a year, twelve have the most population. Of the twenty-one states that pay under $5,000, twelve have the least population. Of the eleven states that pay between $5,000 and $10,000, nine are in the middle range of population. Most states pay legislators an annual salary instead of one based on the number of days, weeks, or months they are in session.

Delaware has the smallest legislature, with 18 Senate and 35 House members. The state has only three counties. Alaska and Nevada are next, with 20 senators and 40 House members or assemblymen. The largest state Senate is Minnesota's, with 67 members. The largest House of Representatives is New Hampshire's with 400 members.

During an average session, a busy state legislature will consider over 4,000 bills, most of them dealing with trivial local matters. A tax bill, or the allocation of school funds, however, can bring a storm of controversy upon the legislature. In addition, there is much pulling and hauling by businesses and professional people—many of them contributors to election campaigns—seeking special legislation for their own interest.

The "one man one vote" decision by the Supreme Court in 1964 caused great changes in the makeup of state legislatures. Before the decision, seats in the House of Representatives, or Assembly, were allocated on the basis of population, whereas those in the Senate represented an overall geographic area. Consequently, there were wide differences in numbers of people represented by different senators.

Since the court ruling, legislatures have been changed so that seats in both houses represent certain numbers of people. Efforts have been made to assure fairly equal representation for the individual voters in every part of each state.

The inequities that existed before the Supreme Court decision usually worked against urban dwellers, who proportionately had fewer senators and representatives in the legislature than those living in rural areas. Many predicted that a massive rearrangement of state government in favor of urban dwellers would follow enforcement of the one man, one vote rule. However, inner cities were losing population, while suburban areas were expanding. Many new legislative districts were assigned to the suburbs, and their representatives often voted the way rural legislators did. As a result, city voters have not received as many benefits as they expected from the change.

The state legislature is the door through which many men enter politics and then rise to higher office. The story of John O. Pastore of Rhode Island is a case in point. His father and mother were born in Italy. The father, a tailor, died when John was nine. For three years while attending school, young John did the housework. His mother and an older brother earned a living for the family. Then his mother married his father's brother, also a tailor. After school, John delivered coats and suits made by his stepfather. During summers, young Pastore ran errands, worked as an office boy, and worked in a jewelry factory. He studied law at night while doing a full day's work as an insurance claims adjuster, then set up a law office in the family home.

Mr. Pastore told a local party leader that he would like to go into politics. Soon, he had his party's nomination to the state Senate and was on his way. After two terms in the legislature, he became assistant attorney general in charge of criminal prosecutions. The next rung on the ladder was lieutenant governor, after which came three terms as governor—and then the United States Senate.

In Missouri, Warren E. Hearnes entered the state House of

Representatives in 1950 as a young man with a law degree. After four terms, he became secretary of state; next came the governorship. Daniel J. Evans of Washington, a civil engineer, went to the state legislature in 1957, served two terms as his party's floor leader, spent a year rounding up support, and became governor of Washington in 1964.

Edward W. Brooke, Jr., also got his start at the state level. Grandson of a Pullman porter, son of a Veterans Administration lawyer, Mr. Brooke grew up in a segregated community in Washington, D. C. He was an officer in an all-Negro regiment in World War II, and emerged from the war with a medal. Settling in Boston, he studied law at Boston University and ran for the state legislature in both the Democratic and Republican primaries. At this point, he became an accidental Republican. The Democrats denied him a nomination. The Republicans gave him a place on their party ticket. From this point, he vaulted into the post as state attorney general, served two terms, and wound up with the Senate seat vacated by Leverett Saltonstall, descendant of a famous New England family, and became the first Negro in the U.S. Senate since the Reconstruction period after the Civil War.

Samuel Ervin, U.S. senator from North Carolina, started his political career with three terms in the legislature. Fred R. Harris, senator from Oklahoma, ex-chairman of the Democratic National Committee, a farm boy, part-time janitor, and printer's helper, also began as a state senator. Milton R. Young of North Dakota, grain farmer and landowner, served a twelve-year apprenticeship in the state legislature before becoming a U.S. senator. John C. Stennis of Mississippi served in the legislature, later was a district attorney and a judge, and then went to the U.S. Senate.

In the effort to move to the upper strata of politics, there always is a chance that a losing candidate will draw enough attention to himself to win an appointment from his party to a good job or gradually make himself well enough known in his state or district to get elected on a later try for office.

An example is the career of William Proxmire of Wisconsin.

He was educated at Yale and taught at Harvard while getting his master's degree. He worked as a student clerk with J. P. Morgan & Company in New York, served with counterintelligence for the army in World War II, then was a newspaper reporter and political columnist. Next he was elected to the Wisconsin legislature. He ran for governor and lost; ran again and lost; ran a third time and lost. By then, most Wisconsin voters knew his name, and when he next ran for the U.S. Senate, he won.

Ralph Yarborough of Texas had a losing record comparable to Mr. Proxmire's before reaching the U.S. Senate. Having been a lawyer, teacher, assistant state attorney general, and district judge, he ran for the post of state attorney general and lost. During World War II, he dropped out of politics to serve as a captain in the army of General George S. Patton, Jr., in its smashing drive across France into Germany. Back home after the war, Mr. Yarborough mustered his resources and ran three losing campaigns for governor before he finally was elected to the Senate.

In New Jersey, Robert B. Meyner, son of a loom fixer, worked his way through school as a newsboy, grocery clerk, garage mechanic, foundry handyman, and tutor until he earned his law degree. Mr. Meyner lost his first try for the state Senate, lost a race for the House of Representatives, finally won election to the state Senate, and stayed in the legislature until picked by the leaders of his party as a candidate for governor. He served two terms as governor for a total of eight years, dropped out for eight years, and tried unsuccessfully for a comeback in 1969.

Gaining office may have its difficulties, but those that follow may be no less trying. One of these, as indicated, is the painful and embarrassing dilemma of limiting the price a politician must pay to the men in the background who, by covering his election costs, made it possible for him to become a governor, a senator, or something else.

Tom Adams, as mentioned earlier, preferred to drop his race for the governorship of Florida rather than pay the price being asked for "campaign money." Having done so, he was free to speak out and disclose what had been involved. What of the many who, by agreeing to run, are not free to speak? This involves a problem of deep concern to an increasingly restless electorate.

CHAPTER NINE

/ **At the Top: The National Level**

In its latter days, the Continental Congress became a forgotten institution in America. Members forgot to attend sessions; there were months when it sat idle for lack of a quorum. States forgot to pay the members who did attend. Everyone forgot congressional requests for money to meet national needs.

James Madison, a young member from Virginia, tried in vain to get funds from his state to cover his own expenses. Like many other members, he survived only through the kindness of Haym Salomon, a Jewish banker in Philadelphia who loaned some $354,000 to individual members and to the Congress itself to handle their most urgent needs. He asked for no interest. Without these loans, the new government would have been crippled. But virtue is its own reward: Mr. Salomon was never repaid, his heirs' claims never reimbursed, not even to the extent of a proposed gold medal honoring their progenitor's contribution to the young nation.

Long before the token settlement was dishonored in 1893, the close ties that linked members of Congress to the states had been broken. Congress set itself free from the states when, under the new Constitution, it became its own paymaster. This put members of the Senate and the House of Representatives in a unique position, speaking for their states and congressional districts, winning their elections from the people back home, but fixing their own salaries and appropriating the money for them.

The 100 senators and 435 members of the House of Representatives today draw equal pay—$42,500 a year. The Senate and the House have relatively equal powers. If the Senate has a louder voice in foreign relations and the approval of important appointments, this is balanced by the fact that tax and spending bills must originate in the House. There is no "upper" or "lower" House of Congress. In the late 1920s, House Speaker Nicholas Longworth took pleasure in giving a lecture to press association editors if he caught such an error in one of their stories. No newsman who ever heard one of Mr. Longworth's lectures on the equality of the two Houses, delivered in his cool Harvard accents, ever forgot it.

The basic rules for Congress are spelled out in the Constitution. Senators must be thirty years old and United States citizens for nine years. House members must be twenty-five years old and citizens for seven years, and every candidate must be a resident of the state from which he is elected. Senators are elected to six-year terms, so staggered that one-third of the Senate is elected every two years; representatives are elected for two-year terms. Each house is the judge of the election returns and qualifications of its own members and determines its own regulatory procedures, such as the selection of officers and the hours of meeting.

Congress added certain laws to control election and campaign expenses for its members. However, these laws apply only to the general election campaigns. Congress leaves the manner of nominating candidates for the Senate and House in the hands of the parties in the fifty states. There, candidates for Congress are selected by the parties in the same way as are governors and local officials.

Each state, regardless of its size, elects two national senators. This was a part of the agreement worked out when the Constitution was written. The grant of an equal voice in one branch

How 435 Members of the House Are Divided Among the 50 States

Note: U.S. Representatives are assigned to the states on the basis of population. House members are limited by law to 435. The estimated current ratio is one Representative for each 479,000 persons.

What We Pay Our Top Officials

(Annual Salaries)

EXECUTIVE BRANCH

President	$200,000
Vice-President	$ 62,500
Top Staff Positions	between $ 60,000 and $ 36,000

LEGISLATIVE BRANCH

Speaker of the House	$ 62,500
President Pro Tem (Senate)	$ 55,000
Majority and Minority Leaders	$ 55,000
Members of Congress	$ 42,500

JUDICIAL BRANCH

Chief Justice	$ 62,500
Associate Justices	$ 60,000
Judges of U.S. Court of Appeals	$ 42,500
Judges of U.S. District Courts	$ 40,000

Source: U.S. Civil Service Commission.

of Congress helped to persuade the smaller states to join the Union. It was taken for granted that senators would speak for states as entities. In *The Federalist Papers,* letters written anonymously by Alexander Hamilton, John Jay, and James Madison and printed in contemporary newspapers to persuade the separate states to approve the new constitution, it was explained: "The equal vote allowed to each state is at once a constitutional recognition of the portion of sovereignty remaining in the individual states and an instrument for preserving that residuary sovereignty."

In line with this idea, senators were chosen by state legislatures until adoption of the Seventeenth Amendment in 1913. Since that time, they have been nominated by their parties in primaries or conventions to engage in the final contest in general elections in November. Because of their clear identity with the state as a whole, senators are more closely allied with their state party than are House members.

The number of representatives allotted each state is determined by its proportional share of the national population, a determination that is reviewed after each federal census. When the size of a state's delegation is changed, the local legislature redefines its congressional voting districts.

Until 1910, each new census brought an increase in the number of seats in the House of Representatives, threatening to make the legislature unmanageable. After 1910, the number of representatives was fixed at 435 but protests were so loud from states that would lose House seats as a result of new census figures that the House of Representatives for years ignored the constitutional requirement that it redistribute its members among the states. Finally, reapportionment came in 1930, when Congress put into effect a measure providing for automatic redistribution of seats after each census. In fixing the boundaries of these new districts, the party in control of the state legislature often tries to arrange them so as to win a majority in more districts than the other party, a process known as "gerrymandering," after its alleged originator, Elbridge Gerry, an early governor of Massachusetts.

Actually, more than three-fourths of the seats in the House of Representatives are fastened so securely by this careful geographic grouping within the congressional districts that they remain largely under control of the same party in election after election. Of 435 House seats, only 90 have shifted from one party to the other during the last five elections. Only 7 of the 38 seats in California have changed parties during this period, 4 of the 11 in Indiana, 2 of the 12 in Massachusetts, 3 of the 15 in New Jersey, 2 of the 27 in Pennsylvania, and 2 of the 10 in Wisconsin.

In 1968, fifty-one House seats were so securely nailed down in California, Massachusetts, Texas, Georgia, and thirteen other states that the incumbents had no opposition at all.

Representatives are expected to reflect the views of the people in their congressional district. This means they must get to know—and to woo—many strangers because a congressional district rarely conforms to that of any other political subdivision. It is larger than any state legislative district, larger than a ward in a city, and, more often than not in the case of a rural district, contains several counties.

At the outset, politicians often have to make it on their own. They rise through the ranks of their party, secure a reputation that reaches across their district, collect a group of supporters, and then launch their candidacy for Congress.

In most cases, it is difficult for an aspiring newcomer to defeat an entrenched congressman. Often he must wait until the officeholder retires or dies. When there is a good prospect of victory, there is no dearth of candidates. When the chances are slim, a party often must beat the bushes to find a candidate, not necessarily because men and women are unwilling to try but rather because they are unable to find supporters who will invest money in what appears to be a losing cause. When both money and party support are forthcoming, candidates sometimes produce surprising victories, unseating even strongly entrenched members of the House.

When a person becomes a member of either chamber of Congress, he literally enters a new world. He is a kind of ambassador to the federal government from his own state or district. Yet he has to keep in mind the welfare of the nation as a whole as well as that of his people at home. He lives and works by rules which are unique. Each house shapes its rules to fit its own needs; is jealous of its own authority and keeps its own secrets.

In the Senate, where the states have equal strength, the vote of a member from Nevada is just as important as that of a member from New York. Each senator is dealt with individually, as an apparent equal, by presidents, pressure groups, and lobbyists. He is always a target for special appeals, entertainment, flattery, and favors. If he is chairman of an important committee, the pressure to persuade is still greater.

In the House of Representatives, where members are more numerous, party leaders usually have key people in each state delegation who serve as a sounding board. These men are consulted before a measure is moved toward a vote. In the House, as in the Senate, committee chairmen hold special places of privilege. Except for the Speaker, no one can match the influence of the chairman of the Ways and Means Committee, which writes tax legislation, or of the Appropriations Committee, which decides expenditures. These men deal in billions of dollars.

Senators who belong to the party occupying the White House usually are consulted about important appointments in their states: federal judges, district attorneys, marshals, and similar officials. House members have a hand in choosing postal officials in their districts. Many members of both houses complain that civil service has left them so few jobs that patronage does them little good.

A House member said: "It is hard to tell who should get a postal job. After you make the appointment, you have one ingrate and fifteen enemies. Nobody seems satisfied with the way you handle it." [1]

---

[1] Clapp, Charles L. *The Congressman: His Work as He Sees It.* Washington, D.C.: Brookings Institution, 1963. p. 102.

Another member said: "Patronage is unpleasant because we have such small bones to toss to people. Party workers of all kinds write and expect we can do something to reward them." [2]

Cut off from home, House members use patronage and favors large and small to build a personal organization for themselves in the home district. They write letters, send Christmas cards, receive visitors, entertain constituents—and keep the big contributors in mind. Many maintain homes and offices both in Washington and in their district. Usually their office in the home district is in the federal building.

Many members of both houses—some of whom have been in Washington for more than thirty years—maintain their ties with and income from their old law offices, now run by partners who prosper because of the name of the Senate or House member attached to the firm. This is no new custom. Daniel Webster, as representative and then as senator from Massachusetts, often tried cases before the United States Supreme Court.

In any sharp disagreement with either the judiciary or the executive departments, Congress holds an important advantage. It alone has the power to levy taxes, decide how money is to be spent, or declare war. Although the three departments of government are equal in theory, Congress holds the whip hand. Many a time, it has driven a hard bargain with a president before giving him the money or legislation that he wanted.

To get things done in Congress, even when his own party holds a majority of the seats in both houses, the president must bargain with committee chairman and individual members. Nowadays, every president has his own group of lobbyists spread through the executive departments, reporting to the White House and keeping in touch with senators and representatives who handle legislation dealing with the executive branch. It is the most powerful lobbying group in Washington because it speaks with the authority of the president. Its argu-

---

[2] *Ibid.*, p. 101-102.

ments are reinforced by the power of the White House to juggle money and jobs into and out of congressional districts and states.

However, despite his bargaining power, a president has no real control over Congress. Unlike England, where the prime minister leads his own party on the floor of Parliament, a president is separated from Congress by the clearly prescribed provisions of the Constitution. The president can negotiate with Congress and with the leaders of his party in Congress but he cannot issue commands.

Spokesmen for the two national party committees have even less power than a president in dealing with members of Congress, even though the party may help finance election campaigns. Senators and House members resent dictation from outsiders. In the Eisenhower years, Paul Butler, chairman of the Democratic National Committee, created a policy committee of prominent Democrats, including Adlai Stevenson, who led the party in two presidential campaigns. The policy committee was snubbed by congressional leaders. House Speaker Sam Rayburn and Democratic Senate Leader Lyndon Johnson refused to attend meetings. Later, when Mr. Johnson was president, Republicans set up a somewhat similar committee of which former President Eisenhower was a member. The group produced a collection of policy statements that were heartily ignored by Republicans in Congress.

Even inside Congress, there is no real party control. In party battles during the 1920s over tariff bills and other hotly fought issues, Democrats and Republicans in both houses of Congress held party caucuses in which they agreed on a party position. Party members were bound to vote for the decision agreed upon by a majority of the party in the caucus. Those who violated the agreement were relegated to unimportant posts on meaningless committees, such as the Committee on Disposition of Useless Executive Papers. But this committee disappeared long ago, and so did the caucus system as a method of enforcing party policy. The last effective use of the caucus was by John Nance Garner when he was Speaker in the early 1930s. By the 1940s Democrats were so widely divided that only the most careful diplomatic negotiations by Speaker Sam Rayburn could bring the North and South together on important issues. By the 1960s the Republicans showed signs of similar divisions.

In part, these divisions in Congress simply reflect the fact that there is not a truly unified Republican or Democratic party because neither has any real control over its widely differing constituent parts which make their own rules in the fifty states. Strange situations develop from this lack of control and cohesion. Democrats were the ones who fought hardest and yelled loudest against the Vietnam policies of a Democratic President, Lyndon Johnson. Republican President Nixon also has had trouble with dissenters in his party.

Rarely is an effort made in Congress to punish a member who refuses to support his party's presidential candidate. An exception was the case of two southern Democrats who bolted the Lyndon Johnson ticket in 1964 to support Barry Goldwater. They were stripped of their seniority on committees—a cherished treasure because seniority means prestige and power. One of the members so punished went home, waited a while, and was elected governor. The other resigned from the House and was reelected as a Republican. Angry Democrats had urged Speaker Rayburn to permit such action against southern Democrats who refused to support the Kennedy-Johnson ticket in 1960. Mr. Rayburn took the position that voters in a congressional district were free to elect any person they wished to represent them. He declined to go along with punitive actions against members.

Often, a more subtle punishment is applied by the national party organization: Members of Congress who consistently refuse to vote with their party leaders are denied campaign money and help from national party headquarters.

In spite of pressures, members of Congress make their own decisions on many issues. It is on taxes, the location of government agencies, jobs, government contracts—the bits and pieces of legislation that give people a chance to make or save money

—that the greatest stress is felt. In these areas, most members vote for what they believe their constituents want.

One member said:

> My first duty is to get reelected. I am here to represent my district. This is a part of my actual belief as to the functions of a Congressman

Another member had this to say:

> You have a responsibility not only to yourself but to your constituents to get reelected. The functions of your office that can legitimately be used to help you get reelected should be used. At least one-third of our activities today are spent in working toward reelection. You know the saying, "you can't be a statesman unless you get elected."

A third member added:

> I want to serve the people. I have been trained for this work. I can do a good job. What I say in a campaign has little to do with my actions in office. How can I serve if I cannot get elected.

A senator who grew up in a political family put it this way:

> Papa used to tell me: "When you are running you are running to get elected." That's what I do. I say and do whatever is necessary. When I get into office, I forget about the oratory and do the best I know how to do.

Through the years, many members of Congress come to feel that the country would go to pieces if they were not reelected. They trim their sails and follow the polls. They take soundings from people back home, especially those who put up the money for campaigns; and they run and run and run.

In many ways, Congress is like a club. Those who win a solid place in the club usually stay for a long time. They trust each other. They give their word in bargains—and keep it. The greatest sin a politician can commit is to break his word in a promise given to another politician. To do so is to fall into the class of man described by former Governor Earl Long of Louisiana: "You can't buy that man, but you can rent him pretty cheap."

Friendships reach across party lines. One of the closest friendships in Washington for many years was that between the Republican Speaker Longworth and John Nance Garner who was to succeed him. Mr. Longworth was a Republican from Cincinnati's aristocracy; Mr. Garner was a roughhewn, plainspoken Texas Democrat. In later years, two House members from North Carolina, Republican and Democrat, rode together daily to their offices. Then the state legislature combined the two districts into one and the two men had to run against each other. The friendship lasted in spite of the campaign, but one had to leave Washington.

The trust given inside the club to a man whose merit they have tested can go to highly undemocratic extremes. Long after the event, Speaker Rayburn told this story:

> General George Marshall and Secretary of War Henry Stimson came quietly to my office one day during the war [World War II]. They brought a scientist with them and explained what they had in mind. They wanted to make an atomic bomb and said the Germans already were working on such a project. But they could not go before a congressional committee and explain the project. It had to be kept secret. They needed $800 million to start the work.
>
> I called in some of the committeemen and told them that $800 million were needed for the war. That was all the members of the committee knew about it and it was all that the House knew. They did not ask any questions. That was all the information the House had on which to appropriate $800 million. The work was started.

Mr. Rayburn had been a member of the club for a long time. The other members took him at his word. When Senator Everett Dirksen of Illinois was in a somewhat similar situation and important issues were at stake, his colleagues in both parties also felt they could depend on him.

Unless his record is in the disaster class, the odds are in favor of a congressman's keeping his membership in the club. This is true to such an extent that during the last generation, at least one House member won reelection while confined with a mental illness from which he never recovered. Another was reelected while serving a prison term.

If alive and breathing, the congressman is better known in his district than the man running against him. He has done favors for constituents that will be remembered at the polls. He has free mailing privileges that his opponent does not have. He has staff members in his district and in Washington to help in the campaign. As an officeholder, he has easy access to newspapers, television, and radio stations. Many members of Congress send out a regular column for small newspapers in their district. They also send back taped interviews and speeches for use on local television and radio stations. The clack of typewriters is heard constantly on Capitol Hill as secretaries keep in touch with congressional constituents.

Said one member:

> Unless you keep constantly in contact with your people, serving them and letting them know what you are doing, you are in a bad way.
>
> My experience is that people don't care how I vote on foreign aid, federal aid to education and all the big issues, but they are interested in whether I answer their letters and who is going to be the next rural carrier or the next postmaster. Those are the things that really count.

Despite the edge held by the man in office, it is still expensive for him to hold his place—it can cost up to $1 million to win a race for the United States Senate in almost half of the states. A hotly fought contest for a House seat in any big-city district can cost from $25,000 to $200,000. In a suburban area, the price range may be from $15,000 to $75,000. Rural seats come cheaper. Costs run from $4,500 to $15,000, depending on the quality of the competition.

Senators and House members in closely contested areas usually have their personal finance committees for campaigns. These are composed of lawyers, bankers, businessmen, union officials. They are relied on to tap the sources of money in the district. Often these personal finance committees arouse the ire of county and local party people who are looking for money from the same sources.

These finance groups have another duty in addition to raising money. They are expected to handle the campaign spending in such a way that there will be no technical violations of the law. The money is spent through special committees whose work is coordinated with that of the candidate. Receipts and spending are filed separately by these committees and are not included in the totals reported by the candidate.

The Federal Corrupt Practices Act of 1925 limits the campaign spending of candidates for representative to $2,500 and that for senator to $10,000. These amounts may be raised to $5,000 for a representative and $25,000 for a senator, depending on the number of votes cast in the district or state in the preceding election. The total is figured at three cents a vote. There have been campaigns in which from five to ten times this amount was spent for each vote.

Spending and contributions must be reported to the clerk of the House of Representatives and the secretary of the Senate, but no official is designated to enforce this requirement, to study the reports after they come in, or to take any action if the law is violated. It would be difficult for the Justice Department to take action since it is a part of the executive branch, and Congress is a law unto itself.

Primary elections are not covered by the federal act, and special committees working at the local level inside a state are not required to report to Washington what they have done. Inside the states, most laws controlling the spending for candidates are ineffective. They apply only to the spending by the candidate and his own committee. Rather than get involved in the legal technicalities, most congressional candidates leave these matters to their campaign managers. Often members of Congress do not know how much has been spent or what promises have been made by their managers. They try hard not to know.

In a study of the operation of congressional offices, including elections and campaigning, Charles L. Clapp produced some interesting figures and observations, published by Brookings Institution in a book called *Congressman*. He cited a member of Congress from an eastern city who said that the amount required to win in his district exceeded the legal limit.

The congressman maintained:

> I don't believe you can be elected in some of these districts, mine included, within the spirit of the law. You can do it within the technicalities. What we had to do was technically legal—we created a whole slew of committees, each one of which would take over a portion of the campaign. I honestly didn't have control of that. I had to run the campaign for the party in my area. My campaign . . . ran over $60,000.

A similar view was expressed by an urban member from the West. He said:

> If you include the costs of the primary I . . . spent about $60,000 last time. . . . One of the senators in my state spent at least $1 million. . . . Legally speaking he would be limited to somewhere around $30,000 (actually $25,000). Now it is obvious that you cannot cover a large state like ours . . . for $30,000. . . . You couldn't put on an advertising campaign for selling dog food in one city for the amount.

Methods and costs vary widely from area to area, Mr.

Clapp found.

A midwestern member reported that he had spent less than $5,000, of which 40 percent came from his own pocket. Except in one city, there were no paid precinct workers in his district. These got $10 on election day and were paid by the party organization.

An eastern member said: "I only spent about $2,00. The party organization puts out county literature and supplies precinct workers. . . . It pained me to spend that $2,000 because most of it comes out of three or four pockets. I have no widespread fund-raising campaign."

On the other side of the coin, losers have a difficult time. One losing candidate spent several years paying off $12,000 of campaign debts from his salary. A local finance chairman was caught in the same way, with $6,500 of campaign debts that he had to pay personally. He said:

> The money is needed during a campaign and you pay it out, expecting to repay yourself, but it never comes in. If you win, you can call up a few people the next day and they're happy to come through with several hundred dollars each to clean up the deficit. If you don't win, you're the lonesomest fellow in the world.

In recent years as political campaigns have grown more expensive, the big money managers have gone more deeply underground. Few members of Congress care to explore the sources or the handling of campaign funds, fearful of what might be discovered. In the more open days of the late nineteenth century, when so many American fortunes were made, the relationship between politicians and financial backers was easier to see. Many a man who dealt in railroads, oil, meat, land, machinery, or sugar, had his own spokesman in Congress and became rich. So did many politicians. The present link between millionaire and politicians is not always so obvious, yet the fact remains that many billions of dollars are spent casually at all levels of government, and new millionaires continue to bob up on the scene.

Politicians often find themselves dealing with issues in which they have a financial interest. Some men withdraw when there is a conflict between their own interest and that of the public. Some do not. A few instances illustrate this point.

Senator Russell B. Long of Louisiana was chairman of the Senate Finance Committee when it considered whether to trim the 27½ percent tax allowance for oil depletion. The senator agreed with oil spokesmen that a reduction in the allowance "would be a breach of faith by Congress."

Within a few days, the Associated Press carried a report from Baton Rouge that of the $1,196,915 of income the senator had from oil and gas leases during the preceding five-year period, $329,151 was free from federal income taxes because of the depletion allowance. The senator was quoted as saying:

> Most of my income is from oil and gas. I don't regard it as any conflict of interest. A long time ago, I became convinced that if you have financial interests completely parallel to your state, then you have no problem. My state produces more oil and gas per acre than any other state in the Union. If I didn't represent the oil and gas industry, I wouldn't represent the state of Louisiana.

A somewhat different view was taken by Representative Thomas S. Kleppe of North Dakota when he disclosed that he owned stock in forty-six companies and nineteen kinds of municipal bonds for a total worth of $3,514,942. Mr. Kleppe, a former mayor of Bismarck and past treasurer of his party in North Dakota, is on the board of directors of a Montana oil company and a Bismarck bank. He said there was a chance of a conflict of interest on legislation affecting these two firms.

"If a bill comes to the floor to end—or cut back the oil depletion allowance, I would decide to vote 'present' unless I decided to resign from the board of [the oil company]," said

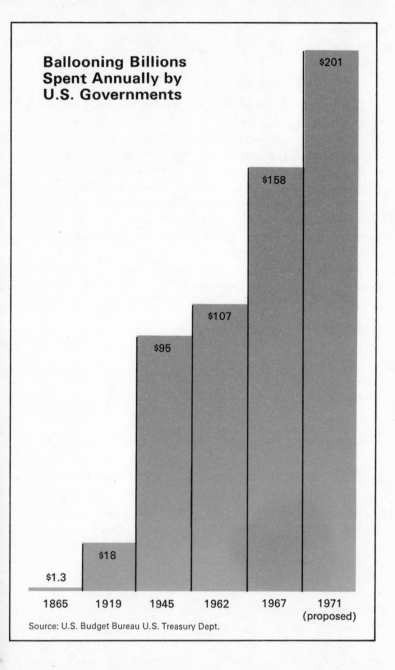

**Ballooning Billions
Spent Annually by
U.S. Governments**

$201

$158

$107

$95

$18

$1.3

| 1865 | 1919 | 1945 | 1962 | 1967 | 1971 (proposed) |

Source: U.S. Budget Bureau U.S. Treasury Dept.

Mr. Kleppe. He declared that he would do the same with respect to banking legislation.

Senator Long and Representative Kleppe are not alone in such situations. There are many others whose sources of income are less visible. But reform must wait until Congress agrees on a stricter code of ethics which it is willing to enforce. Until then, there is little likelihood that the voting behavior of members will change when it comes to what is considered to be a conflict of interest between themselves and the public they are elected to serve.

CHAPTER TEN / **Grand Prize: The White House**

Leap Year affords an extraordinary opportunity in more than one respect. It is a time when any native-born citizen, at least 35 years of age, may run for president of the United States and bid for one of the great prizes of the world: the White House.

No one in his thirties has yet won the White House. The youngest president was Theodore Roosevelt, who came in through the back door at 42 when William McKinley was assassinated. John F. Kennedy at 43 almost tied the record. Only five other presidents reached the apex of politics while still in their forties: Ulysses S. Grant, hero of the Civil War, at 46; Grover Cleveland, governor of New York, at 47; Franklin Pierce, a senator, at 48; James K. Polk and James A. Garfield, both seasoned politicians, at 49.

Under the American system of separation of powers and of checks and balances, the presidency is one of the three principal pillars of government. He who occupies the White House shares national power with members of Congress and members of the Supreme Court. Congress makes the laws; the president, as head of the executive branch of government, carries them out; and the Supreme Court decides whether they square with the Constitution and therefore are to be considered valid.

The purpose of this system, of course, is to prevent any one person or group of persons from securing too much power and undermining the balance on which free and constitutional government rests. James Madison wrote: ". . . the accumulation of all powers, legislative, executive, and judiciary, in the same hands . . . may justly be pronounced the very definition of tyranny."

While each of the three branches has been accused at different times of encroaching on the powers of the other, the great changes produced by an age of exploding scientific development has necessarily expanded the authority of the president enormously. For example, the advent of nuclear weapons makes it virtually essential to confer on the president the unlimited and unilateral power to retaliate against a nuclear attack on this country. There would be no time to secure the advice and consent of the Senate or to debate the issue before the Supreme Court if nuclear retaliation were considered essential for survival of the nation.

Even in the absence of nuclear conflict, the powers of the president have grown in recent years in the area of foreign affairs. Congress alone has the right to declare war, yet the president can involve the country in war without a declaration. Vietnam is a recent and striking instance.

The powers of the president—expanded or contracted by the course of history—are outlined in the Constitution. The president is commander-in-chief of the armed forces. In conducting the nation's foreign affairs, he may make treaties with other countries, subject to approval of two-thirds of the Senate. He appoints ambassadors to foreign posts and receives those assigned to Washington. He also appoints judges and public officials, many of whom are subject to Senate approval. He may grant reprieves or pardons for certain federal crimes. He prepares an annual budget charting the spending of billions of dollars. Congress then examines the budget and has the last word as to how much shall be spent for what.

As in the case of lesser offices, those who pretend to the presidency must run two races—one to secure the nomination and the other to win a general election. And since the stakes are the highest in the land, the extent of the effort which must be made and the importance of the money factor are proportionately higher.

With few exceptions, it is estimated that at least two to four years of concentrated effort together with large sums of money are needed for a serious campaign to win a presidential nomination. Richard M. Nixon invested four years in his 1968 nomination. It took John F. Kennedy nearly five years to put together and to execute his successful strategy for securing a majority at the Democratic convention.

Work on Franklin D. Roosevelt's nomination began a good two years before the 1932 convention. Immediately after Mr. Roosevelt had been reelected as governor of New York in 1930, Mr. Farley—then state Democratic chairman—sent a little booklet to state chairmen, vice chairmen, national committeemen and other party workers around the nation. The booklet gave a little information about the party in New York State, and, was intended to spark a correspondence between Mr. Farley and party workers across the country. After that, a tabulation of Mr. Roosevelt's vote in the 1930 election, simply comparing it to that of other Democrats, was sent to the same people.

At the same time, financial backers were approached, and support was secured from a number of prominent men, including Frank C. Walker, a New York lawyer; Henry Morgenthau, Sr., a former ambassador; William M. Woodin, an industrialist; William A. Julian, an Ohio businessman; Edward J. Flynn, Democratic leader of the Bronx; Jesse I. Strauss, a New York merchant; Herbert H. Lehman, banker and lieutenant governor; Joseph P. Kennedy, a man of many business interests; Robert W. Bingham, a Louisville publisher; Edwin W. Pauley, a California oil man; Richard Reynolds of the North Carolina tobacco family.

The first campaign money came in during March, 1931, a full year before the presidential campaign began to warm up. That spring, campaign headquarters were opened in New York City, and letters went out to party workers. Men and women, including personal friends of the prospective candidate, were enlisted to direct the work and to help get delegates. Roosevelt scouts, unsalaried but with their expenses paid, moved through the Rocky Mountain and southwestern states to recruit delegates. Mr. Farley and Louis Howe, another skillful strategist, worked steadily.

In July, 1931, Mr. Farley made a trip across the country. The ostensible purpose was to attend an Elks convention in Seattle. Along the way, he talked with important party people in eighteen states, listening, collecting information, making a pitch for his candidate. He sent reports back to Mr. Roosevelt. Later, Mr. Farley figured that he met 1,100 party people on this trip. By autumn of 1931, the preconvention organization was ready. Plans were set for the primaries, and the rest is history.

The Goldwater drive began in early October, 1961, three years in advance of the 1964 election. F. Clifton White, a New York public relations man with an acute sense of politics, and three friends invited twenty-two men from sixteen states to meet in Chicago. They formed a central planning group with Mr. White as chairman to win the nomination for Mr. Goldwater. Most of the men were veterans of World War II. Two were members of the House of Representatives. Three were Republican state chairmen and most of the others also held important party posts.

Mr. White gave the group a course in practical politics. He told them how to build an organization from the precinct up and how to plan the selection of delegates from their districts and states. While other politicians sought to pick off the top party leaders in their states, Mr. White's group was working to get their men on committees at the bottom of the party. A state chairman later remarked: "We are having people show up in district conventions that we never heard of and know nothing about. The party is being taken over by people who are strangers to us. We don't know where they are coming from." [1]

In the early spring of 1962, thirty members of Mr. White's group spent two days at a hunting lodge in Minnesota developing plans for the struggle to come two years later. The White group was ready to pick the state chairmen, finance chairmen, and women's leaders for their campaign in each state. As the plan unfolded, Mr. White came up with a leader for the Goldwater movement in every county and congressional district in the country. A detailed study was made of the way in which each state chose its delegates to national conventions. Regional directors were told to master the state rules and make certain that their state chairmen were familiar with them. Every detail had been covered by the time the first calls for precinct meetings went out in January, 1964.

The national convention is the supreme authority of both major political parties. However, it meets only once every four years, and then only briefly, leaving the management of party affairs to delegated officers the rest of the time. Its outstanding function is the nomination of the party's candidate for president and vice president. This lends great importance to the selection of delegates to the national convention.

In view of this vital function, it might be supposed that there would be widespread popular interest and vigilance in the selection of delegates. Yet it is estimated that 97 percent of the voters have no participation in the selection of two-thirds of the delegates who are sent to national conventions to nominate presidential candidates.

The rules of each national party, revised regularly, determine the number of convention delegates allocated to each state. Basically, each state is given twice as many delegates as its number of electoral votes—that is, two delegates for

---

[1] White, F. Clifton. *Suite 3505*. Arlington House, New Rochelle, New York, 1967.

each senator and representative in Congress. This figure is enlarged by "bonus" delegates awarded to states which produced good-sized votes for the party in a preceding election.

State laws determine how delegates are chosen. In the great majority of states, parties choose their delegates by conventions or through committees. In the other states, including the most populous ones, delegates are chosen in state presidential primaries.

In the case of the thirty-five states which use the convention method, the choice of delegates starts at the precinct level. The precinct chairman calls a meeting of party people to elect delegates to a county or congressional district convention which, in turn, picks delegates to the state and national conventions. In many cases only six or eight people show up for the precinct meeting, mostly active party workers and spokesmen for the men who finance the cost of party operations. At the state and district meetings a few weeks later, delegates to the national convention may or may not be instructed to vote for a particular presidential candidate, depending on how much pressure has been applied to the dozen or so people who actually run the party in the state and district. In these states, the average voter has nothing to say about which candidate his own state delegation will support. If state leaders are committed to a man, they frequently arrange for the selection of local and state delegates who will support him.

Twenty of the thirty-five states using the convention method have laws regulating the holding of precinct meetings. In these states, the voter who keeps his eyes and ears open can find the meetings and attend them. He is likely to be regarded by the regular party people as a tourist rather than as a participant.

In eleven of the thirty-five states, precinct meetings are held at the call of the precinct chairman. The call usually is heard only by those dedicated party workers who happen to be within whispering distance. In a few states and areas, attendance is fairly good, but in the others, surveys by the

Allocation of Delegates to National Political Conventions

	Republican Party	Democratic Party		Republican Party	Democratic Party
Alabama	26	32	Montana	14	26
Alaska	12	22	Nebraska	16	30
Arizona	16	19	Nevada	12	22
Arkansas	18	33	New Hampshire	8	26
California	86	174	New Jersey	40	82
Canal Zone	—	5	New Mexico	14	26
Colorado	18	35	New York	92	190
Connecticut	16	44	North Carolina	26	59
Delaware	12	22	North Dakota	8	25
Dist. of Col.	9	23	Ohio	58	115
Florida	34	63	Oklahoma	22	41
Guam	—	5	Oregon	18	35
Georgia	30	43	Pennsylvania	64	130
Hawaii	14	26	Puerto Rico	5	8
Idaho	14	25	Rhode Island	14	27
Illinois	58	118	South Carolina	22	28
Indiana	26	63	South Dakota	14	26
Iowa	24	46	Tennessee	28	51
Kansas	20	38	Texas	56	104
Kentucky	24	46	Utah	8	26
Louisiana	26	36	Vermont	12	22
Maine	14	27	Virginia	24	54
Maryland	26	49	Virgin Islands	3	5
Massachusetts	34	72	Washington	24	47
Michigan	48	96	West Virginia	14	38
Minnesota	26	52	Wisconsin	30	59
Mississippi	20	24	Wyoming	12	22
Missouri	24	60	**TOTAL**	**1333**	**2622**

League of Women Voters, the National Municipal League, and the Survey Research Center at the University of Michigan show the percentage of voter participation to be around three percent. There seem to be too many precincts for effective regulation or policing—3,500 in Chicago, 4,000 in Indiana, 2,900 in Kansas, 9,300 in Pennsylvania, 5,500 in Texas.

In the remaining four states of the thirty-five—Arkansas, Georgia, Louisiana and Rhode Island—Democratic party rules were so fixed until 1968 that no ordinary party voter could have a voice in choosing delegates. In Arkansas, the state committee which selected delegates to the 1968 convention had been chosen by state conventions held in 1966, two years before. Georgia delegates were selected by the Democratic state executive committee; often they were handpicked by the governor from among his friends. Louisiana delegates were named by the state party committee. Rhode Island followed a similar practice. Arkansas Republicans followed the same practice as the Democrats. In Georgia, Louisiana and Rhode Island, Republicans used state conventions to name delegates to the national convention.

This meant that the largest number taking part in the selection of delegates to nominate a Democratic candidate for president in these states was only 61 in Arkansas, 15 in Georgia, 105 in Louisiana and 204 in Rhode Island. Voters, of course, theoretically held the power to vote precinct and county leaders out of office, but that required great popular activity.

In 1967, the League of Women Voters called on its members to attend precinct caucuses and to learn what was happening. The effort was keyed to the 1968 presidential election. The women accordingly sought out half-hidden precinct meetings, and examined the candidates for election to precinct committees. A few samples of what they found help to point up the general situation in convention states.

In Arizona: A county committeeman trying to broaden attendance once sent out 500 invitations to registered members of his party asking them to come to a meeting at which the process of choosing delegates to the national convention would begin. Only twelve voters showed up.

In Colorado: Typical attendance at a caucus was six or eight persons. This small group elected a committeeman and a committeewoman and picked a delegation to the county convention. This was the organization at the grassroots. Out of it came the raw material that produced delegates to the national convention.

In Idaho: Delegates to the county central committee were elected two years in advance of the presidential election.

In Maine: Only about 2 percent of the voters of either party attended caucuses.

In Minnesota: Only half of one percent of eligible voters had gone to precinct meetings in 1966. These had named precinct officials for two years, along with delegates to county and congressional district conventions.

In New Mexico: There were times when county chairmen forgot to call precinct meetings. They simply picked their own delegates to county conventions.

In Washington: The chairman of King county (Seattle) was accused of keeping secret the places where caucuses were to be held. In another county, League members were denied a list of precinct meetings. The *Seattle Times* warned that no caucuses would be held in some counties and party officers would remain in office indefinitely.

In Wyoming: Party people generally named the delegates.

Members of the League of Women Voters came to the conclusion that they could have little influence unless they joined party organizations and really worked at being politicians. In one precinct in Texas enough women attended a meeting to take command. They voted to oust the precinct chairman. The next morning they went to the courthouse to record their action. They met the ousted chairman on the courthouse steps. His reelection had already been recorded. The women had been too late.

Presidential primaries offer little solace to the voter.

At one time or another, twenty-four states have used the

alternative of presidential primaries to elect delegates to party conventions. By 1968, the number had been reduced to fifteen states and the District of Columbia. In most of these states, voters have a chance to express their preference about the presidential candidates of their party. The states still using the primary method of selecting delegates are California, Florida, Illinois, Indiana, Massachusetts, Nebraska, New Hampshire, New Jersey, Ohio, Oregon, Pennsylvania, South Dakota, West Virginia, and Wisconsin. In Alabama, this system is used only by the Democrats. Through the years, the primary has been tried then abandoned by Georgia Democrats as well as by Iowa, Michigan, Minnesota, Montana, New York, North Carolina, North Dakota, and Vermont.

In very few cases has a primary victory been a deciding factor in the nomination of a presidential candidate. Nevertheless, primary elections sometimes have been very helpful. For example, Richard Nixon made use of the primary in 1968 to show Republicans that he commanded considerable voting strength notwithstanding earlier setbacks. It helped him shed the "loser" tag after he lost a presidential race and a bid to become governor of California. John F. Kennedy's primary victories in 1960 also nailed down his party's nomination for him. The Democratic big-city bosses remained on the sidelines until they were convinced that his victories, especially in West Virginia, indicated that the country would accept a Roman Catholic as president.

A presidential candidate goes into a primary only when he must. He sometimes needs publicity to make himself better known or an opportunity to present his ideas to the public. Or he needs backers who are willing to gamble a million dollars or so on the long chance that he can become president. He then must select a few states that are best calculated to give him primary victories. Usually, he avoids a direct confrontation with his principal opponent for the nomination.

Yet even if a candidate wins in a primary election, delegates in several states are not bound to cast their ballots for him in the national convention.

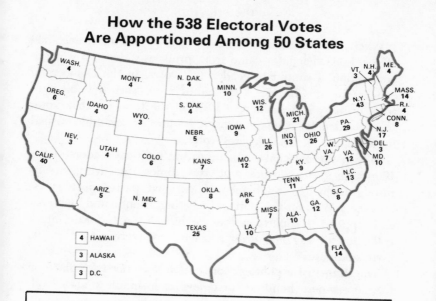

How the 538 Electoral Votes Are Apportioned Among 50 States

WASH. 4
OREG. 6
MONT. 4
IDAHO 4
N. DAK. 4
S. DAK. 4
MINN. 10
WIS. 12
MICH. 21
VT. 3
N.H. 4
ME. 4
MASS. 14
R.I. 4
CONN. 8
N.Y. 43
PA. 29
N.J. 17
DEL. 3
MD. 10
NEV. 3
UTAH 4
WYO. 3
NEBR. 5
IOWA 9
ILL. 26
IND. 13
OHIO 26
W. VA. 7
VA. 12
CALIF. 40
COLO. 6
KANS. 7
MO. 12
KY. 11
N.C. 13
ARIZ. 5
N. MEX. 4
OKLA. 8
ARK. 6
TENN. 11
S.C. 8
GA. 12
MISS. 7
ALA. 10
TEXAS 25
LA. 10
FLA. 14

4 HAWAII
3 ALASKA
3 D.C.

Demography of the Vote in Recent Presidential Elections

(by percentages)

		Sex		Race		Youth Voters (Under 30)	Union Labor
		Men	Women	White	Non-White		
1948	Republican	44*	47*	47*	19*	38	26
	Democrat	56*	53*	53*	81*	62†	74†
1956	Republican	55	61	59	39	57	43
	Democrat	45	39	41	61	43	57
1960	Republican	48	51	51	32	46	35
	Democrat	52	49	49	68	54	65
1964	Republican	40	38	41	6	36	—
	Democrat	60	62	59	94	64	—
1968	Republican	43	43	47	12	38	29
	Democrat	41	45	38	85	47	61
	Wallace	16	12	15	3	15	10

*Figures accompanied by an asterisk are taken from Angus Campbell et. al., *The Voter Decides* (Row, Peterson, 1954), pp. 70-71. All other data are taken from releases of the American Institute of Public Opinion (The Gallup Poll).
†Includes Democratic, Progressive, and States' Rights votes.
Source: Gallup Poll.

When the Republicans met in 1968 at Miami Beach, 509 of the 1,333 delegates came from primary states. To win the nomination, a candidate needed 667 votes. In the Democratic convention at Chicago, 1,106 votes were cast by delegates from primary states whereas 1,312 of the total of 2,622 votes were needed for a nomination. A traditional scramble ensued for a majority of the delegates' votes.

It is at the national convention that political leaders of the 100 state parties work out the diplomatic arrangements through which a semblance of national party unity is established. Without this national meeting, chaotic and turbulent as it appears, the party system might easily deteriorate into a collection of regional groups, each endeavoring to elect its own candidate.

The drama of a political convention does not take place on the floor where hundreds of delegates assemble under floodlights and cameras. The decisive events occur in private clubs and hotel suites, in quiet meetings of political leaders from the various states. This is where the decisions are made which determine the outcome of the voting on the floor.

Long before a convention meets, the framework for the nominating decisions has been devised by party leaders. If a party does not hold the White House, convention arrangements are made long in advance by the national committee after consultation with spokesmen for the presidential candidates. If the party does hold the White House, a presidential staff decides who is to run the convention and its various committees. Mrs. Faye Broderick of Maine was elected chairman of the Committee on Permanent Organization for the 1968 Democratic convention. On paper, her committee had the responsibility of choosing the chairmen of three important convention committees. Mrs. Broderick found, when she got to Chicago, however, that the other committees had already been at work and their chairmen had been installed. The real decisions had been made at the White House. Her committee could only register its formal approval.

Though key decisions often are completed before they arrive at the convention city, delegates and their alternates, staging mob scenes in hotel lobbies and on the convention floor, feel that they are an important part of history in the making. They talk with delegates from other cities and states, and return home fired up for the campaign ahead. Whatever may be its faults, the national convention is the only place where members of the fifty separate party units come together for a national rally. At this one time every four years, they give an appearance of being members of one party.

The real choice of a presidential candidate lies largely in the hands of a few party leaders from states with big blocks of delegates. California, Illinois, Michigan, New York, Ohio, Pennsylvania, Texas can be keys to an election. The appraisal by party leaders from these states is important because they know by polls and other means whether a candidate will be accepted by the voters in their states. Furthermore, they know just how hard it will be to raise money for a candidate. While holding their delegations together, they argue, deal and negotiate until a decision is reached. Then the delegates vote.

From the sidelines, a presidential campaign appears filled with glamor. A candidate comes sailing in on a jet airliner. He is met by a cheering crowd at the airport, tours the city in a limousine, followed by cars and buses filled with party people and newsmen. He makes a speech. There are more cheers and smiles. Pretty girls carry banners, go through fancy marching routines and whoop it up. Then the candidate and his entourage zip away to go through the same routine in another city hundreds of miles away. He may visit five or six cities a day and put on the same show before he crawls wearily into bed in the early hours of the morning. He follows this same routine day after day through the months of September and October.

Behind the whoop-la is a carefully planned and precise strategy developed by men who spend endless hours in a central headquarters miles away. These men are rarely seen.

What It Costs to Keep the President In the White House
(Annually)

Salary	$ 200,000
Expense allowance	50,000
Travel allowance	40,000
Special-projects fund	1,500,000
Budget for the White House	3,229,000
Secret Service and White House police	2,503,000
Maintenance of White House grounds	200,000
Maintenance of White House aircraft, ships, and automobiles, and pay of crews and chauffeurs	1,000,000
Auto leasing fees (estimated)	50,000
TOTAL COSTS	**$8,772,000**

Estimated capital value of certain properties available to the President

The White House estate	$125,000,000
Aircraft	30,000,000
Naval vessels	500,000
Camp David	150,000
TOTAL	**$155,650,000**

Source: USN&WR

The schedule for the plane, the parade, the speech and the trip back to the airport has been timed to the minute. The enthusiastic crowds do not appear by accident; they are arranged by an advance man whose job it is to prepare for roaring "impromptu" receptions. Local supporters provide the cars and buses. Party leaders are instructed to be present at the rally. Mimeograph machines on the plane turn out copies of the speech for newsmen. Stories are filed, broadcasts prepared. The speeches are produced by professional writers, touched up here and there by the candidate. The pretty girls are hired from modeling agencies; they smile and wave for any candidate who pays their fee. By the end of the second week, the candidate and everyone else in the entourage is bone-tired. From that time on, they move and talk in a daze.

Lawrence F. O'Brien—rated by some professional politicians as the smartest campaign manager since James A. Farley helped put Franklin Roosevelt in the White House—worked out an organizational plan for handling such an operation. The plan evolved from Mr. O'Brien's work in the campaigns of John F. Kennedy, Lyndon Johnson, and Hubert Humphrey. It was composed of these elements:

- At the top, a campaign manager who may speak for the candidate, issue statements, and sign advertisements.
- Next, a campaign director who has the complete confidence of the candidate and the campaign manager. Responsible for success or failure of the campaign, he organizes and supervises the campaign committee, finds a finance chairman, a press secretary, and the key members of the campaign team. He has complete control over spending. He chooses the site for campaign headquarters and coordinates the work of special campaign groups with that of the party's national committee. He selects a field director to work with local party leaders in checking registration drives, distributing materials, listening to reports and complaints, sending them back to headquarters. The field director travels the nation.
- A finance chairman, chosen because of his knowledge of people willing to invest money in the election of a president.

How the Nation Voted in Six Presidential Elections

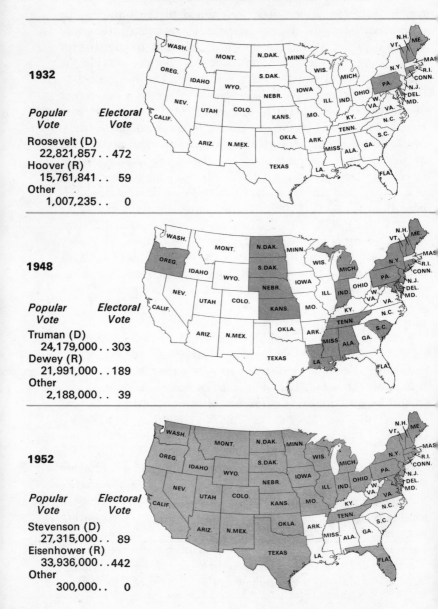

1932

Popular Vote	Electoral Vote
Roosevelt (D) 22,821,857	472
Hoover (R) 15,761,841	59
Other 1,007,235	0

1948

Popular Vote	Electoral Vote
Truman (D) 24,179,000	303
Dewey (R) 21,991,000	189
Other 2,188,000	39

1952

Popular Vote	Electoral Vote
Stevenson (D) 27,315,000	89
Eisenhower (R) 33,936,000	442
Other 300,000	0

1960

Popular Vote *Electoral Vote*

Kennedy (D)
  34,227,000 . . 303
Nixon (R)
  34,108,000 . . 219
Other
    503,000 . . 15

1964

Popular Vote *Electoral Vote*

Johnson (D)
  43,130,000 . . 486
Goldwater (R)
  27,178,000 . . 52
Other
    337,000 . . 0

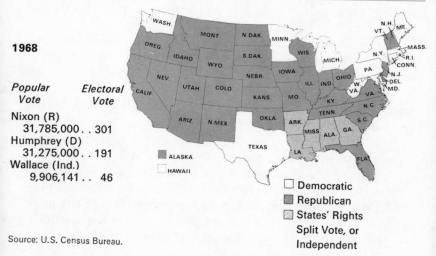

1968

Popular Vote *Electoral Vote*

Nixon (R)
  31,785,000 . . 301
Humphrey (D)
  31,275,000 . . 191
Wallace (Ind.)
  9,906,141 . . 46

☐ Democratic
■ Republican
▨ States' Rights
Split Vote, or
Independent

Source: U.S. Census Bureau.

He channels money to the various committees created to avoid a violation of the Corrupt Practices Act, and selects the staffs who arrange testimonial dinners, clambakes and the sale of campaign materials.

• A press relations man, usually a journalist, who directs the preparation of material for newspapers, television and radio. He understands reporters and how they work, knows the men with whom he is dealing.

• A specialist assigned to plan campaign schedules for the candidate. Travel details are worked out, airplanes are rented and reservations made long in advance.

• Writers and researchers who produce speeches after the general topic and basic approach have been discussed with the candidate. Usually, the candidate can deliver speeches pretty much as they are written.

• Local committees and headquarters, established in key states and cities.

• Special committees, created for veterans, young people, the aged, labor, farmers, professional people. The ideal campaign organization ranges across the full economic and social spectrum, so these committee chairmen are frequently chosen from appropriate ethnic groups.

• Thousands of volunteers, enlisted to work under the direction of the professionals.

One of the founding fathers wrote in 1788 that the method of electing a president was one of the few sections of the Constitution that had received even slight approval from opponents of the document.

The unique method, like almost everything else in the Constitution, was a compromise. A bow to the small states was made by giving each state a number of electoral votes equal to the total number of members it had in the two houses of Congress, one electoral vote for each senator and one for each representative. This gave the small states a little more influence in electing a president than if the number of electors had been determined on a basis of population. And a part of the agreement that calmed their fears and induced them to come into the Union. Except for minor patchwork, that portion of the Constitution has remained unchanged. Each state is free to choose its presidential electors in any way it sees fit.

By long-established custom—not by law—the presidential candidate receiving the largest number of votes in a state is given all of the electoral votes of that state. It is conceivable in a three-way contest that the popular votes might be divided among the candidates in such a way that one got 33 percent, a second 32 percent and the third 35 percent— and that the candidate with 35 percent would get all of the state's electoral votes.

There are many scare stories about what would happen if a third-party candidate managed to throw a presidential election into the House of Representatives.

Realistic politicians suggest that nothing much would happen except that one of the two major party candidates would be elected president by the House. No third party candidate has ever had more than a few House seats. The minor party candidate would have neither the votes in the House nor the party machinery needed to take over the government.

Through the years, proposed changes have taken three principal forms.

• One would divide the electoral votes of a state among candidates according to the proportion of popular votes each candidate received.

• A second would give the electoral votes of each congressional district to the candidate getting the most popular votes in that district. The two electoral votes awarded each state for its senators would go to the candidate polling the largest number of popular votes in the state as a whole. Such a plan has been tried by several states, including California, Kentucky, Maryland and West Virginia, but has always been abandoned after several elections.

• A third plan would provide for the popular vote of presidents by the nation as a whole. Many object strongly to such a proposal on the grounds that it would go far toward destroying the two-party system since the whole party structure is built around the concept of state and local governments.

Despite protest, however, the original idea is still in force. Two elections have been thrown into the House of Representatives where, after much travail, a president was elected. One election was decided by a special electoral commission. On several occasions, a president has squeaked through with a majority of electoral votes but with fewer popular votes than those secured by his opponent. There were angry words and flaring tempers, but the nation survived, and plans for revising the electoral system were set aside for another day.

CHAPTER ELEVEN / **Register**

In the complicated world of politics and government, citizens often find themselves frustrated, wondering what they should do. There is no overnight remedy, but there are several important things that every citizen can do:

1. Register. This is one of the first major steps to active full-time citizenship.

2. Vote regularly. If the voter likes none of the candidates, he may vote against the man in office. By throwing out incapable officials, voters can force parties to produce competent candidates.

3. Become a "stockholder" in government and play the political game. This means learning the basic rules of politics, talking with neighbors, giving money and effort to a favorite party and candidate.

These steps may sound familiar, yet the fact is that only a handful are presently involved in selecting our political leadership. This and following chapters seek to clarify the simple duties of citizenship which could improve the political picture.

The first step a citizen takes to have a voice in government is putting his name on the list of registered voters in his community. Until this is done, he is a non-functioning citizen in the eyes of his neighbor; to the politician, he simply does not exist.

A person is eligible to register if he is a citizen of the United States, has lived a specified time in his voting precinct, and is deemed an adult by the laws of his state. In most states, if he meets these standards, all that is necessary is to find the proper local official and ask to have his name put on the voting lists. He signs his name and becomes a qualified voter.

Yet, despite the ease of enrollment about one of every four adults in the United States is not registered. In presidential years, such as 1968, the proportion of unregistered voters drops to 23 percent.

Census Bureau studies estimate that twenty-six persons out of each hundred men and women of voting age will not be registered for the 1970 elections to choose a new Congress, many governors and state officials, along with thousands of county and local office-holders.

Of the twenty-six who are not registered, two are not citizens. Five have not lived in their new homes long enough to meet residence requirements. The remaining nineteen have a variety of excuses for failure to put their names on the voting lists: They are not interested. They just could not get around to the registrar's office. They cannot be bothered. They do not know why they are not registered. Some have no excuse at all. In the total registration picture, the Census Bureau found in 1968 that almost 3 million persons did not even know whether they were registered.

More than 12 million young people become eligible to vote for the first time in each election year. On the basis of registration figures, however, those who find the most wrong with society in the United States today are making the least effort to accomplish any legitimate change. At last count, 40 percent of voters between the ages of 21 and 25 had failed to put their names on voting lists—about double the number of non-registrants in any age bracket over 35. These non-registrants include 39 percent of the young men and 41 percent of the young women.

Registration climbs as the young move out of their mid-twenties and settle into full-time jobs and professions. Many of those under thirty-five list residence requirements as the reason for not registering. This is particularly true of college graduates, who move around more frequently than those with little education.

In order to register or vote, a person must be 21 in all states except four. Georgia and Kentucky have reduced the voting age to 18 which conforms to the age at which a young man is eligible to be drafted for the armed services. Alaska fixes the voting age at 19 and Hawaii at 20.

All states require a voter to have lived in the state, county and precinct for a certain period of time. One reason for this is to make certain that a person has been in the state long enough to be familiar with local issues and customs before permitting him to vote.

The length of time varies from three months in New York and Pennsylvania to two years in Mississippi. Fifteen states require six months of residence. Thirty-two states and the District of Columbia require one year.

However, more than half the states have special provisions to allow persons who meet all other requirements except those of residence to vote in presidential elections. Both new and former residents may vote for president in Alaska, Arizona, Connecticut, New Jersey, Texas and Wisconsin. Former residents may vote in Vermont and Wisconsin. New residents may vote in twenty-five other states. These are:

California	Illinois	Michigan	New York
Colorado	Kansas	Minnesota	North Carolina
Delaware	Louisiana	Missouri	North Dakota
Florida	Maine	Nebraska	Ohio
Georgia	Maryland	New Hampshire	Oklahoma
Idaho	Massachusetts	New Mexico	Oregon
			Washington

There are many variations in residence requirements. Quite

a few states—among them Alaska, California, Colorado and Connecticut—specify that residence is neither gained nor lost while living in an institution maintained by the state.

In all states, there is an interval just before election in which registration is not permitted. The time ranges from a few days in some states to fifty-three days in California. This period is used to get the lists of qualified voters prepared for use by election officials and party people on election day.

In most states, registration takes on an air of permanency. Once a person's name is enrolled on the voting lists, it remains there if he votes with any degree of regularity. Mrs. Elizabeth Yadlowsky of the American Law Division at the Library of Congress combed through the registration requirements of the fifty states and produced the following analysis.

Two states, Alaska and North Dakota, have no requirement for registration.

Nine states have no specification that a person must vote at certain intervals to keep his name on voting lists after he has registered. Registration is permanent. These states are: Alabama, Colorado, Connecticut, Maine, Massachusetts, Mississippi, New Hampshire, Vermont and Virginia.

Nine states require a person to vote in every general election to keep his name on the books. These are: Arizona, California, Idaho, Montana, Nevada, New York, Oregon, Utah and Wyoming.

Three states demand that a person vote in every primary and general election: Hawaii, Indiana and Kentucky.

Three states require a vote in one of the two preceding general elections: Delaware, Nebraska and New Mexico.

Six states keep a registrant's name on the books if he has voted once in any election in the last two years: Florida, Louisiana, Michigan, Ohio, Pennsylvania and Wisconsin.

West Virginia requires one vote during a period in which two primary and general elections were held.

Georgia drops a registrant's name off the list if he has not voted once during the previous three years.

Nine states demand a vote once every four years to keep a

citizen's name on the registration lists. They are: Arkansas, Illinois, Minnesota, Missouri, New Jersey, Oklahoma, South Dakota, Tennessee and Washington.

Two states call for one vote during every five-year period to ~~maintain an~~ enrolled status. They are Maryland and Rhode Island.

North Carolina requires one every six years.

Texas demands annual registration.

Kansas requires registration for each general election.

Iowa calls on the voter to re-register every presidential election year.

South Carolina demands a fresh registration of all voters every 10 years.

There was a time when roving bands of hired voters moved from one precinct to another to vote over and over again. In New York, for example, boatloads of voters were hauled up and down the Hudson river to drop ballots in precincts along the way. This is why all but two states now require voter registration.

Today, a check list of those qualified to vote is kept at the polls. As each voter appears, his name is checked against the list. He signs his name or a mark is made beside his name to show that he has voted. Poll-watchers are employed to guard against repeaters.

However, this method is not fool-proof. Registration lists are not always up to date. The names of those who have died or moved away since the last election are not always removed promptly from the lists. Party people sometimes use the names of the absent or the dead to build up the votes for their candidates. This is easy to do, when there are not enough poll-watchers for the opposition party.

Because of this possibility, permanent registration, although a convenience to the voter, lends itself to voting frauds. In crowded areas where election officials do not know by sight those who apply for the right to vote, there is always the danger that improper ballots will slip through. France devised a method to prevent this. Each voter who went to the polls

Minimum Residence Requirements
For Voting in State and Local Elections

	In State	In County	In Precinct
Alabama	1 year	6 months	3 months[1]
Alaska	1 year	None	30 days
Arizona	1 year	30 days	30 days
Arkansas	1 year	6 months	30 days
California	1 year	90 days	54 days
Colorado	1 year	90 days[1]	20 days
Connecticut	6 months	6 months in town	None
Delaware	1 year	3 months	30 days
Dist. of Col.	1 year	None	None
Florida	1 year	6 months	45 days
Georgia	1 year	6 months	None
Hawaii	1 year	3 months	3 months
Idaho	6 months	30 days	90 days for county seat election
Illinois	1 year	90 days	30 days
Indiana	6 months	60 days in township	30 days
Iowa	6 months	60 days	10 days for municipal and special elections
Kansas	6 months	None	30 days
Kentucky	1 year	6 months	60 days
Louisiana	1 year	6 months	3 months[1]
Maine	6 months	3 months in city or town	None
Maryland	1 year	6 months	6 months[1]
Massachusetts	1 year	None	6 months
Michigan	6 months	30 days in city or township[1]	None
Minnesota	6 months	None	30 days[2]

Minimum Residence Requirements

(continued)

	In State	In County	In Precinct
Mississippi	2 years	None	1 year
Missouri	1 year	60 days	None
Montana	1 year	30 days	None
Nebraska	6 months	40 days	10 days
Nevada	6 months	30 days	10 days
New Hampshire	6 months	6 months in town[1]	None
New Jersey	6 months	40 days	None
New Mexico	1 year	90 days	30 days
New York	3 months	3 months	3 months
North Carolina	1 year	None	30 days[1]
North Dakota	1 year	90 days	30 days
Ohio	1 year	40 days	40 days
Oklahoma	6 months	2 months	20 days
Oregon	6 months	30 days	30 days
Pennsylvania	90 days	None	60 days in district
Rhode Island	1 year	6 months in town or city	None
South Carolina	1 year	6 months	3 months
South Dakota	1 year	90 days	30 days[1]
Tennessee	1 year	3 months	None
Texas	1 year	6 months	None
Utah	1 year	4 months	60 days
Vermont	1 year	90 days in town[1]	None
Virginia	1 year	6 months	30 days
Washington	1 year	90 days	30 days
West Virginia	1 year	60 days	None
Wisconsin	6 months	None	10 days[1]
Wyoming	1 year	60 days	10 days[1]

[1]If less may vote in old precinct.
[2]If less may vote in old precinct if in same municipality.
Source: U.S. Senate, Office of the Secretary, *Nomination and Election of the President and Vice President of the United States* U.S. Government Printing Office, January 1968. Corrected to September 18, 1968.

was required to produce an electoral card bearing his full name, profession and residence. Each card was numbered and could be compared easily with the official list of voters.

The practice of removing from registration rolls the names of voters who are absent, dead or disqualified for some other reason differs from state to state. A few states required a house-to-house canvass of adults in populous areas. About three-fourths of the states permit an interested voter to challenge the right of others to vote; only a few states permit the registrar to make such a challenge. About half of the states provide for transmission of official death notices to voting officials. A few states have a similar requirement in the case of insanity or conviction for a major crime. But in most states the business of purging registration rolls of dead, absent or disqualified voters is a hit-or-miss affair.

The clearest provisions for keeping polling lists up to date are found in New Hampshire and Vermont. There, voting officials are required to review and revise the lists before each general election. Many other states charge registration officials with this duty but provide them with neither the money nor the facilities with which to do the work.

Twenty states allow voters to enroll without applying in person at a registrar's office. The prospective voter simply writes to the proper county official requesting an affidavit of registration which he fills out and returns. Nine other states permit such registration by persons who are ill or physically handicapped. Nineteen do not allow absentee registration.

Of the forty-eight states requiring registration, nine waive this formality for those in the armed forces—Kansas, Missouri, New Jersey, Oklahoma, Ohio, Rhode Island, Texas, Virginia and Wisconsin. Two states—Alabama and Louisiana—do not allow absentee registration by servicemen. The remaining thirty-seven states permit servicemen to file an absentee registration. In a few cases, they may file for registration at the same time they send in absentee ballot.

Registration is facilitated in many states. Offices of registration officials are open on all business days except during a specified period in advance of an election. Some states, such as Florida, Arkansas and California, permit the registrar or supervisor of elections to designate deputies who open registration books in precincts as needed.

In other states, the process is trickier. Registration offices in Maryland are open only two days a month. Delaware voters may register in even-numbered years on the fourth Saturday of July, and second Saturday of September and third Saturday of October.

Registration in Connecticut takes place during a two-hour period once a month except for the time between the sixth and fourth weeks before elections. On the last weekday before election, the Boards for Admission of Electors are required to meet to register those who have met the age, citizenship and residence requirements during the last days before an election.

In New Hampshire, the Board of Supervisors of each town compiles a list of the voters. Regular sessions are held to correct this list by adding new registrations or removing the names of those who have moved or otherwise are not entitled to vote.

Electoral requirements are often more informal in rural areas of the Middle West stretching out to the Rocky Mountains. Colorado permits any qualified voter who is known to the county clerk to register other members of the family who live at the same address.

Iowa requires registration in cities of 10,000 or more; smaller towns may require registration if they choose to do so. Registration is not required in the rural areas of Kansas, Nebraska and Wisconsin. It is optional in the less populous areas of Ohio and Missouri.

In the long run, statistics indicate that education has much to do with registration. Professional people are more likely to register than any other group. Eighty-eight percent of these men and women are enrolled as voters. Next are white-collar workers with 85 percent. Down toward the bottom of the list are those who work for wages. Only 62 percent of these are

Minimum Residence Requirements For Voting in Presidential Elections

	President and Vice President only (For recent movers to the State)		President and Vice President only (For recent movers to the State)
Alabama	Not applicable	Minnesota	30 days
Alaska	No minimum	Mississippi	Not applicable
Arizona[1]	60 days	Missouri	60 days
Arkansas	Not applicable	Montana	Not applicable
California	54 days	Nebraska	No minimum
Colorado	6 months in State, 90 days in county, 15 days in precinct	Nevada	Not applicable
Connecticut[1]	60 days	New Hampshire	30 days
Delaware	3 months	New Jersey[1]	40 days in county
Dist. of Col.	Not applicable	New Mexico	30 days in county
Florida	30 days	New York[1]	30 days in election district
Georgia	30 days	North Carolina	60 days
Hawaii	Not applicable	North Dakota	No minimum
Idaho	60 days	Ohio	No minimum
Illinois	60 days in election district	Oklahoma	No minimum
Indiana	Not applicable	Oregon	No minimum
Iowa	Not applicable	Pennsylvania	Not applicable
Kansas	45 days in township or precinct	Rhode Island	Not applicable
Kentucky	Not applicable	South Carolina	Not applicable
Louisiana	Not applicable	South Dakota	Not applicable
Maine	30 days	Tennessee	Not applicable
Maryland	45 days in ward or election district	Texas[1]	60 days
Massachusetts	31 days in city or town	Utah	Not applicable
		Vermont	Not applicable
		Virginia	Not applicable
		Washington	60 days
		West Virginia	Not applicable
		Wisconsin[1]	No minimum
Michigan	No minimum	Wyoming[1]	Not applicable

[1]State permits former residents to vote for President and Vice President where not qualified in new State of residence.

Source: U.S. Senate, Office of the Secretary

registered—about the same as for unemployed persons.

The less education a person has, the smaller his desire to vote. Only 56 percent of those with a fourth grade education are registered. In terms of income, only 68 percent of those earning less than $3,000 a year are registered. As earnings pass the $10,000 mark, the number of registrants rises to 84 percent.

Rigid literacy tests as a requirement for voting were barred by the 1965 Civil Rights Act. It substituted the simple obligation that a person demonstrate that he had the equivalent of a sixth grade education before being permitted to register.

At the time the 1965 Act was passed, 20 states had literacy requirements. Only seven of these states were in the South where such tests were often used to withhold the vote from Negroes. Not only the southern states but quite a few large cities across the nation have found it necessary to revise their qualifications for electors since passage of the 1965 law.

The old law in Alaska required a voter to be able to speak and read English. Arizona, California, Maine, Massachusetts and New Hampshire demanded that a person be able to read the Constitution and write his own name. Connecticut ordered a voter to read the Constitution of the United States and the Connecticut statutes in English. Delaware required a person to read the state constitution and write his own name. Hawaii specified that voters be able to read, write and speak English or Hawaiian. New York and Oregon voters were asked to be able to read and write English. In Washington state, they must be able to read and speak English. Wyoming demanded that they be able to read the state constitution.

Literacy tests in many southern states were more rigid than in most states of the North.

Alabama required a person to be able to read and write any article of the United States Constitution in English. This was changed after the 1965 Act to require a certificate from the board of education that a person had the equivalent of an eighth grade education.

The Georgia law specified that an applicant must read and

write in English the United States or the Georgia Constitution or be of good character and understand the duties and obligations of citizenship under a republican form of government.

Louisiana required that an applicant be able to read and interpret any clause in the United States or Louisiana Constitutions, to be of good character, and to be attached to the principles of the Constitutions of the state and the United States.

The new Mississippi law simply demands that an applicant be able to read and write. This was adopted after the 1965 Act.

North Carolina requires a registrant to be able to read and write any section of the Constitution in English.

South Carolina's law carries an alternative to the literacy test. A person must be able to read and write any section of the state constitution or own and pay taxes on $300 of assessed property.

Virginia requires a person to fill out his registration application in his own handwriting.

Some states with large groups whose native tongue is not English have revised their laws to remove discrimination. In Connecticut, the law was changed to permit anyone to register who had finished the sixth grade whether or not the predominant classroom language was English. New York requires a registrant to be able to read and write in English except for those educated in Puerto Rico. Louisiana, where some only speak Creole French, has always had a law permitting the tests to be taken in a person's "mother tongue."

Six states require a registrant to take a loyalty oath. These are Alabama, Connecticut, Florida, Idaho, North Carolina and Virginia.

Almost all states bar the registration of felons—those guilty of infamous crimes—and insane persons. Most states withhold the vote from convicted criminals until their civil rights have been restored. Colorado and Oregon restore their citizenship automatically on release from prison. Maine and Michigan do not permit them to vote by absentee ballot while in prison. The provision for criminals is broadened in some states to

Higher Education, Higher Registration

Of those of voting age with this amount of education	this percent registered to vote
Elementary School:	
0 to 4 years........	38.4
5 to 7 years........	52.4
8 years........	62.4
High School:	
1 to 3 years........	61.3
4 years........	72.5
College:	
1 to 3 years........	78.4
4 years........	83.1
5 years or more.....	85.7

Performance by Different Occupation Groups

Of those of voting age in this group	this percent registered to vote
White Collar Workers, (Professional, managerial, clerical)...........	79.8
Manual workers....	62.3
Service workers....	62.7
Farm workers......	69.9

Note: All races, both sexes.
Source: U.S. Department of Commerce, 1969.

permit a registrar to refuse to enroll as voters those of "bad character." Among these are Alabama, Connecticut and Mississippi.

Twelve states refuse to allow someone guilty of an offense against the election laws to vote. Alabama bars vagrants and those who make false election returns. Delaware withholds the franchise for ten years from those guilty of election offenses. Hawaii, Maryland, Massachusetts, New Hampshire and New York bar those guilty of corrupt election practices.

Ohio withholds the vote for four years from those guilty of a second offense against the election laws. West Virginia and Wisconsin refuse to enroll persons involved in election bribery.

Pennsylvania withholds the vote for four years from persons guilty of an election offense. In case of election bribery, it does not permit the guilty person to vote in that particular election. Vermont specifically disqualifies "any elector who shall receive any gift or regard for his vote, in meat, drink, moneys or otherwise."

As of 1967, the Idaho law, in addition to the insane and felons, refused to register the following: Those convicted of embezzling public funds; those buying or selling votes; bigamists and polygamists; anyone teaching, advising, counselling, aiding or encouraging any person to enter into such a marriage; and those teaching that the laws of the state are not the supreme law of the state.

Despite various legal complications, few have much trouble getting their names on registration books. Registrars more often than not accept an application as a matter of routine. Few questions are asked.

The most difficult problem remains that of getting people simply to register. They cannot hope for any meaningful influence on government unless and until they bring themselves to take this first basic step.

In ancient Greece, the word *idioces* was used to describe those who refused to hold office. More generally, it applied to citizens who did not vote. The English term "idiot" was derived from this word.

The founders of the American Republic spent months studying the democracy of classical Greece before drafting the Constitution of the United States. They found that voting and holding office were an inseparable part of citizenship. The franchise in ancient Athens was limited to those sons of free Athenian parents who had reached the age of 21. They fought the battles and paid the expenses of government. They were a small group of well-to-do people, about a seventh of the population. The concept of citizenship was that of a man who not only voted but also was ready and able to serve the state at any time. Slaves, women, most of the working men and a large part of the merchant class were excluded from citizenship.

Whereas the right to vote and to full citizenship was highly exclusive in ancient Greece, it has become virtually unlimited and open to all adults in modern America. Herein lies a great problem. In a system limited to a civic-minded and educated aristocracy, the body politic was a responsible one. In a system virtually without limit, it may be highly irresponsible.

The extent to which Americans are irresponsible by failing to register already has been noted. The same irresponsibility extends to in their failure to vote.

One of every three citizens failed to vote in the 1964 presidential election. In 1968, as in all elections in the United States, there were more persons not voting than the number required to reverse the outcome. In 29 states, the number of non-voters, had they gone to the polls and voted for Hubert Humphrey, was large enough to have reversed decisions in favor of Richard Nixon. On the other side of the picture, Mr. Nixon's majority of electoral votes could have been vastly enlarged if non-voters in thirteen states that went against him had gone to the polls and voted for him. Only in Alabama, Hawaii, Massachusetts, Mississippi, Rhode Island and the District of Columbia would they have failed to overturn the pluralities against him.

A Gallup study of the non-voters in 1968 found that:

• 15 million were registered but did not have enough interest to vote.

• 10 million could have registered but did not.

• 7 million were sick or disabled.

• 5 million were prevented from voting by residence requirements.

• 3 million persons were away from home.

• 1 million did not obtain absentee ballots.

The worst ten states in numbers of non-voters were California, Georgia, Illinois, Michigan, New Jersey, New York, North Carolina, Ohio, Pennsylvania and Texas. New York was the highest with 3.7 million non-voters. California, Illinois, New York, North Carolina, Pennsylvania and Texas each had around a million registered who did not take the trouble to vote.

In presidential elections, voter turn-out has ranged from a high of 85 percent in 1876 to a low of 44 percent in 1920.

States With Best and Worst Voting Records

(Voters as percentage of voting age population)

THE BEST

States	1968	1964	1960
Delaware...........	70.0	70.2	73.6
Idaho..............	72.6	76.5	80.7
Indiana............	71.8	73.9	76.9
Iowa..............	70.8	72.4	76.5
Minnesota..........	76.0	76.9	77.0
New Hampshire......	70.0	72.4	79.4
South Dakota.......	72.8	74.4	78.3
Utah..............	76.1	78.9	80.1
Washington.........	71.0	71.8	72.3

THE WORST

States	1968	1964	1960
Alabama...........	50.3	35.9	31.1
District of Columbia...	33.5	39.4	—
Georgia............	42.9	43.0	30.4
Mississippi.........	50.6	33.2	25.5
South Carolina......	45.9	38.7	30.5
Virginia...........	50.4	41.1	33.4

Source: Census Bureau.

How U.S. Voters Compare With Others

Country	Last general election year	Percentage of voting-age population who went to polls
Australia..............	1969..............	94.9
Canada...............	1968..............	75.7
Denmark.............	1968..............	89.3
Finland..............	1966..............	84.9
France...............	1968..............	80.0
Germany.............	1969..............	86.8
Great Britain..........	1966..............	76.0
Ireland...............	1969..............	75.0
Norway..............	1969..............	82.5
Sweden..............	1968..............	89.0
Switzerland...........	1967..............	65.7
United States..........	1968..............	70.5

Source: U.S. Census Bureau and Governmental Affairs Institute.

It was about 61 percent in 1968.

Non-presidential elections always attract less voters, while primaries draw fewer still. In 1966, only 29 million votes were cast in primary elections. About 60 million were counted in the general elections. If this trend continues, more than twice as many will vote in 1970 non-presidential elections as in the primaries.

The net result of a low vote in primary elections is that the choice of candidates is left largely to political leaders. The average citizen who carries the tax load simply fails to speak up on issues that may be of vital importance to him.

The right to vote, now held so lightly that almost one of every four Americans does not take the trouble to sign his name to the voting lists, was won slowly over a period of two centuries by bitter argument and in one case outright rebellion.

Whether a person could vote or hold office once depended on a man's religion, his money or his ownership of land. In the first constitutions adopted after the Revolution, Maryland, North and South Carolina required the ownership of 50 acres of land or the equivalent in money. Pennsylvania had a property tax. South Carolina added to property requirements a specification that a man must be white, believe in God and in a future state of reward and punishment. New York voters had to be freeholders, have their names on a list of tax payers and have a tax receipt. Massachusetts, Connecticut and Rhode Island had property requirements.

New Jersey had a property requirement for voting but the framers of the original state constitution unintentionally left a loophole not found in any of the other states. The document simply specified that a person must own a certain amount of property, be twenty-one and live in the state. For thirty-one years, women, aliens and Negroes were free to vote. In 1807, a new law restricted the vote to free, white, male taxpayers.

At the office-holding level, the original constitutions of Connecticut, New Hampshire, New Jersey and Vermont barred atheists, Jews, free-thinkers, and Roman Catholics from election as governor. Maryland and Massachusetts required that a governor be a Christian and own a certain amount of property or money. The other states adopted requirements such as that a governor believe in the Trinity; or believe in the inspiration of the Scriptures; or be a Protestant; or believe in one God, heaven and hell, and be ready to declare openly that every word of the Bible was divinely inspired. Qualifications for a seat in the state legislature were much the same.

Within ten years after the inauguration of George Washington, seven states had rewritten their constitutions to broaden the privilege of voting and office holding. Pennsylvania wiped out religious tests and every tax-paying male over 21 was given the right to vote. South Carolina opened the polls to Catholics. New Hampshire abolished the poll tax, abandoned religious tests and gave the vote to all men over 21. Delaware abandoned religious tests, gave the vote to all free, white men who had paid taxes and lived in the state two years. Vermont admitted to the polls any man, white or black, who had lived in the state one year. Georgia abandoned property requirements. Kentucky granted franchise to any free, white man.

Kentucky's frontiersmen had set a standard too liberal for their neighbors. Tennessee to the south required a man to own 200 acres of land in the county he represented before serving in the legislature; to be governor, he had to own 500 acres. Indiana, on the other side of Kentucky, gave the vote to all white, male citizens but required a person to be a taxpayer in order to serve in the legislature or as governor.

Gradually, the vote expanded across the eastern states. In 1809, Maryland gave suffrage to all male citizens. Connecticut lowered the tax requirement for voting to a trivial amount in 1818.

Massachusetts was tougher. In 1818, John Adams and Daniel Webster protested against lowering the requirements for voting. Webster said equal suffrage was incompatible with inequality of property and that if property requirements were removed from the voting privilege there would be either attacks by the poor on the rich or a reaction by the rich against the poor. In spite of his reservations, the ban was lifted and the state seemed to survive.

A year later, the fight for voting rights raged through New York. Chancellor James Kent countered: "Universal suffrage never can be recalled or checked but by the strength of the bayonet. . . . If we let go our present hold on the [state] Senate, we commit our proudest hopes and our most precious interests to the waves." He added that universal suffrage when applied to the legislative and executive departments of government had been regarded with terror by men of all ages.

Virginia held out a few years longer. Not until 1830 could anyone other than a landowner vote. Rhode Island property owners held their control of that state until it came to a point of outright rebellion. Thomas Wilson Dorr led an armed revolt in the early 1840s that jarred the state government into granting virtually universal suffrage. North Carolina clung to the property requirement until the Civil War.

The Negro did not arrive on the scene as a full-fledged voter in all states until quite recently. In most states, the vote was restricted to white men until 1870.

In that year, the Fifteenth Amendment to the Constitution sought to enfranchise Negroes in all states, but particularly in the South where most Negroes lived. As a result of an agreement with northern politicians in 1876, however, enforcement of this part of the Constitution was virtually ignored in southern states between 1877 and the early 1960s. Very few Negroes were permitted to vote there.

Even when allowed to register, Negroes were excluded from any real choice among candidates since they were barred from voting in primary elections. Prior to the 1960s, the South had white Democrats who ran things and Negro Republicans who disagreed with them. Important election decisions were made in Democratic primaries. States permitted the parties to set their own rules for choosing candidates. Since there was no Republican party to speak of, Negroes who were registered had no candidates to choose for the general election.

In 1944, the Supreme Court held that "white" primaries were unconstitutional. After that, barriers to Negro voting in the South came down steadily. Civil Rights laws in the early 1960s caused states to change their literacy tests and use of the poll tax was abandoned.

Between 1964 and 1968, Negro registration in the eleven states of the Confederate South rose by almost a million. There were 3.1 million Negroes on the voting rolls there in 1968. This represented 62 percent of the Negroes of voting age as compared to 78 percent of whites. Since the 1940s Negro voting power had multiplied in the South five times.

By 1968, most of the states had moved to make voting easier for all of their citizens. At the request of Congress, arrangements had been made to permit those in the armed forces or overseas on foreign duty for the United States to vote by mail in most states. A few states went so far as to permit such persons to vote in primaries as well as in general elections. Most states also liberalized the laws to permit others away from their home precinct or out of the state to vote by absentee ballot.

Thirty-one states had laws requiring employers to give workers time off to vote without any loss of pay. Many of these laws make the requirement contingent upon whether the voter has enough time during non-working hours to cast his ballot. Indiana and Louisiana go so far as to declare a holiday on election day. Minnesota permits voters to take off the forenoon of election day. Arkansas calls for work stoppage at 4 P. M. on election day. Ohio and Texas provide such reasonable time as is needed. Most of the other states allow from one to three hours.

Nineteen states and the District of Columbia make no such provision. The states are:

Connecticut	Michigan	North Carolina	South Carolina
Delaware	Mississippi	North Dakota	Vermont
Florida	Montana	Oregon	Virginia
Idaho	New Hampshire	Pennsylvania	Washington
Maine	New Jersey	Rhode Island	

In many of the states that make no provision for time off to vote, federal, state and local government agencies allow their own employees to take time to go to the polls. Many labor union contracts also provide for their members to take such time in the absence of a state law.

Almost all elections in the United States are held on a Tuesday in November. Many other nations hold their elections on Saturdays and Sundays. In some countries, the polls remain open longer than the one day provided in the United States. Italy and Switzerland permit voting for one and a half days. Finland allows two days.

In the United States, each state fixes the location of polling places and the hours polls will remain open on election day. Voting hours range from seven in rural Tennessee to fifteen in New York City. Most polling places are set up in public buildings, school gymnasiums, fire houses, police stations, armories, libraries and similar places.

In some states, city and town elections are held in the spring or early autumn so that their own issues will be considered separately from those involved in state and national elections. Louisiana, in a break from the usual custom, elects its governors in February of presidential election years.

The kind of ballots used varies widely from state to state and county to county. In general, two types are most popular —the "party" and the "office-type."

The "party" ballot makes it easy for a voter to select all of the candidates of one political party. In thirty-three states the candidates of each political party are listed in separate rows on paper ballots or voting machines. This helps the voter to find the candidate of the party he favors.

Twenty-seven of these states permit a voter to register his

The U.S. Voting Record
(Millions)

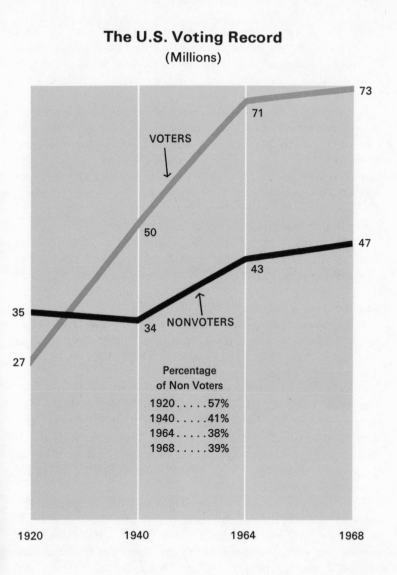

VOTERS

NONVOTERS

73

71

50

47

43

35

34

27

Percentage
of Non Voters
1920 . . . . . 57%
1940 . . . . . 41%
1964 . . . . . 38%
1968 . . . . . 39%

1920   1940   1964   1968

Source: U.S. Bureau of the Census and Clerk of the U.S. House of Representatives

ballot for all candidates of his party by marking an "X" in a circle at the top of the column or by pulling a single lever on the voting machine. Politicians like this plan. It makes voting more difficult for those who want to exercise independent judgment.

If the voter decides to choose his own candidates and divide his vote between the parties, he must go down the list, sorting out his favorite candidates one by one and sprinkling "X's" or pulling levers along the way. He has to be careful not to put an "X" in the circle at the top. He must not make a mistake and vote for two persons for the same office. These errors could nullify his ballot.

Studies of straight-ticket ballots indicate that:

• Many are likely to vote for a whole slate of candidates because this is much easier than thinking about the names of candidates on the lists below. Except for a few names at the top of the ticket, most voters have little knowledge on which to base a judgment about the candidates.

• In states that permit straight-ticket voting, the voters are less likely to break away from their party's presidential candidate than they are in states where they must vote separately for each candidate.

• Independent voters appear to like the straight-ticket form. Most independents take little interest in politics. They vote because of publicity and pressure from their neighbors. The straight ticket makes it easy for them. The Survey Research Center at the University of Michigan reports that as many as 60 percent of independents vote a straight ticket in states where such ballots are used.

Six states use the party-type ballot but do not permit the voter to cast a ballot for the entire ticket by putting one mark in a circle at the top of the list of a party's candidates. It is simple, however, for the voter to go down the list of names and mark his approval, candidate by candidate. It is equally easy for him to change columns and vote for a candidate of the opposite party.

The "office-type" ballot is used in seventeen states. On this, candidates are listed according to the offices they seek. There is no clear line of distinction between parties. The voter is on his own. He must select candidates and parties for each office.

Usually, the most important offices to be filled are listed at the top of the ballot. Candidates for each office are separated clearly from those for another office. The party of each candidate is printed below the name of the contestant.

This ballot makes it harder for a person to vote a straight ticket, especially in states where the names of a party's candidate are not always in the same sequence in the list of contestants. In Ohio, where such a ballot was adopted at the suggestion of the late Senator Robert A. Taft, the names of candidates are rotated according to parties. That is, the name of the Republican candidate for governor may be listed at the top of contestants for that office. In the next group of candidates, the democratic nominee would appear first. All down the list, the voter must look for his own party's candidate if he wishes to vote a straight ticket.

It is not always easy to vote an "office-type" ballot, nor are the votes always easy to count. In Oregon, for instance, the names of candidates are rotated so that no candidate gets first place on every ballot. However, national, state and county offices are clearly separated.

The position of a candidate's name on the ballot can mean the difference between victory and defeat. The same is true of a political party. Many voters endorse a candidate whose name happens to be in a prominent place rather than look for another name. Consequently, men and parties maneuver for the best position.

In states using a party-type or "straight-ticket" ballot, the political party in control of the statehouse usually orders that the names of its candidates be listed in the left-hand columns of the ballots or voting machines. This position is chosen because most people read from left to right across the page. The eyes of the voter fall first upon that side of the ballot.

When an "office-type" ballot is used, the preferred position for individual candidates or a dominant party is at the top of the list of contestants for particular offices. Voters read naturally from top to bottom.

The arrangement of names on ballots comes about in many ways. Some of the methods follow:

• Positioning in some states and counties is left to state and local officials. They have a free hand to give preferred positions to their favorite candidates.

• Candidates in primaries sometimes are listed in the order in which they have filed notice of their candidacy. This occasionally invites collusion between election officials and candidates.

• In some states, candidates and parties draw lots for position.

• Names in a few states are listed in alphabetical order. This gives an advantage to those whose names come near the front of the alphabet. There have been cases in which parties refused to nominate candidates whose names started with letters far down the alphabet because they would have an unfavorable position on the ballot.

• About half of the states follow a custom of rotating the names of candidates and parties on ballots and machines. This tends to give each party an equal advantage. It makes all names equally hard to find.

• Under each office, Massachusetts lists the names of the incumbent, if any, first. After that comes the name of the candidate of the other major party. Any other candidates are listed in alphabetical order. This gives the man in office the advantage of top position in the contest for his particular office.

• Nevada requires that candidates be listed alphabetically, giving an advantage to a man whose name starts with a "B" over a contestant whose name starts with a letter farther down the alphabet. In 1969, by coincidence, the names of the two senators from Nevada were Bible and Cannon and the House member's name was Baring.

• In a few states like Colorado, the position of a candidate's name on the ballot in a primary election is determined by the number of votes he got in the state party convention. That is, the man most favored by the active politicians in his party gets the preferred place on the ballot. Colorado aligns candidates for national office in alphabetical order on paper ballots; on voting machines they are rotated from precinct to precinct.

Many states provide spaces on the ballots for write-in candidates, giving the voter the privilege of supplying his own candidates. However, the write-in vote is rarely effective. Several instances of state-wide approval for a write-in candidate have appeared in recent years. Senator Strom Thurmond of South Carolina was elected in 1954 as a write-in candidate. And in 1964, against formidable opposition, Henry Cabot Lodge won a New Hampshire presidential primary with a write-in vote.

In presidential years, the ballot arrangement varies from state to state. Under the election system, no person votes directly for president and vice president. Instead, the vote is for a slate of electors who are expected to vote for the presidential and vice presidential nominees of their party. In some states, the names of the electors are printed on the ballot. Elsewhere their names are omitted and only the names of the presidential and vice presidential candidates are visible; the electors are so remote that even their names are not seen.

The majority of states use a long ballot which lists not only candidates for office but also widely varying proposals for changes in law. Many of these require the voter to be well-informed in order to vote intelligently.

In some states the ballot is as long and wide as the top of a bridge table. It may contain the names of hundreds of candidates for fifty or more offices as well as complicated explanations of a dozen or so bits of legislation or changes in the state constitution. These referenda are printed in small type. The language is legalistic and obscure. They put the average man in the position of deciding issues he is not qualified to judge. State legislatures have passed a problem along to the voters, often because they were afraid to make a decision themselves. All too often, these legalistic puzzles leave voters with a sense of complete frustration.

In 1968, one state presented the voters a "bed-sheet" ballot with long lists of candidates and referenda, so complicated that even the politicians were confused. It carried fifty-eight proposals for constitutional amendments, twelve to be voted on by all counties in the state, and forty-six others to be decided by the counties they affected.

One state official reported: "When too many of these measures are submitted to the voters at one time, the tendency is just to vote 'no' on all of them instead of taking time to read the lengthy ballot." Many good measures have thus been beaten at the polls.

California often presents the list of candidates for national, state and local offices on a single ballot, along with a long list of referenda on state, city and county questions. The issues can range from a proposed change in judicial procedures at the state level to a technical decision about the legal height of city buildings. But whatever the ballot, the best defense for the voter is to read the instructions at the top of paper ballots carefully or to examine the sample voting machine set up at most polls.

When available, it is also wise to pick up a sample ballot before the election to study the candidates and issues involved, noting decisions and choices on this ballot. Most states permit this material to be taken into the polls to be used as a guide. If not, the voter can always jot down some notes to use inside the booth. In some localities, sample ballots are provided at government expense. In other areas, they are printed by political parties or special interest groups in an effort to persuade voters to support their candidates or their side of an issue on the ballot. This does not necessarily work to their benefit. Many voters use the sample ballot as a road map to find the candidates and issues they want to vote against.

Election materials giving an unbiased checklist of the background of candidates and what they stand for are provided in many areas by the League of Women Voters and may be had for the asking. This service is provided without charge. The League is operated as a community service organization and is always glad to receive contributions.

Some of the ballot reforms that have been proposed to make it easier for the voter to express his will would:

• Broaden the use of voting machines. More than half of all votes are now cast by machines. Almost every state makes some use of them. A few states vote entirely by machines. If any sort of supervision is given, it is hard to juggle the results on them. They are generally noted for speed, accuracy and efficiency.

Rise of Negro Voters in South

	1960	1968		
	Negroes Registered to Vote			
Alabama.........	66,009	273,000	Up	314%
Arkansas.........	72,604	130,000	Up	79%
Florida..........	183,197	292,000	Up	59%
Georgia..........	180,000	344,000	Up	91%
Louisiana........	159,033	305,000	Up	92%
Mississippi.......	22,000	251,000	Up	1,041%
North Carolina....	210,450	305,000	Up	45%
South Carolina....	58,122	189,000	Up	220%
Tennessee........	185,000	228,000	Up	23%
Texas............	226,818	540,000	Up	138%
Virginia..........	100,100	255,000	Up	155%
TOTAL..........	1,463,333	3,112,000	Up	113%

Source: Voter Education Project, Southern Regional Council.

• Abandon the "straight party" ticket used in most states. This makes it harder for the voter to find the names of the candidates he supports, but it gives all candidates a fairer chance.

• Make ballots easier to read. Typography is poor in many states.

• Provide separate elections for national, state and local candidates. This would shorten the ballot, but separate elections would increase costs and would probably bring fewer to the polls to vote for state and local officials.

• Simplify language on ballots and voting machines used to explain the various referenda brought before the public.

• Provide for a wider distribution of sample ballots before elections so that voters can do their homework.

With or without these proposed improvements, the opportunity to vote is there. As indicated earlier, the will, not the ballot, is the ailing factor in the American political system.

CHAPTER THIRTEEN / **Mobilize**

The government you choose keeps germs out of drinking water and bugs out of corn flakes. It puts out fires, picks up garbage, educates children, and guarantees them a fair wage when they grow up. It is involved in health and housing and jobs and recreation. It regulates industry and equips the armed forces. And all of this is in the hands of politicians.

The definition usually applied to the politician is far too narrow. Each citizen has the right to be one. The stream of governmental decisions in the United States is supposed to flow, not down from the high hills like a river, but up from the people like a spring.

On the basis of votes cast in the 1968 elections, 39 percent of the people are not working at their jobs of being politicians, even in a minimal way. If voting in the elections of Governors and Congressmen continues to follow the current pattern, 45 percent of Americans—almost one of every two—will shirk their duty in the future.

When an employer does not put effort into his business, the company fails and he forfeits his investment. Should an employee neglect his job, he loses it. If the American voter fails to open his eyes and act, he could receive a rude shock in the days ahead. There are extremists on both sides who would like to change the American system.

The current state of politics is sharply criticized by some experienced politicians. According to one Republican:

> We have let political involvement become too secondary to our society. As politicians, all of us, Republicans, Democrats, Independents, have failed to excite enough people to stimulate them to take an active part in the civic and political life of this country.

A Democrat said:

> The trouble is that so many people who have brains and knowledge and a big stake in what their communities should desire and seek to accomplish are silent, political cowards. Business leaders in most communities are political cowards, and the result is that they don't communicate to the city hall or to Washington except through some fellow who, they feel, is skilled and paid. They think they can do it with money, as a contribution to a candidate or to an association leader, instead of doing it themselves.

Elmo Roper, a noted pollster, put it this way:

> We are dedicated to the idea of democracy and representative government. The whole theory back of it is that people from different walks of life will be equally motivated to seek elective office and be willing to accept appointive office. That theory has fallen down rather badly. We haven't got people from all walks of life equally willing to run for elective office or accept appointive office.

Unwittingly, the citizen who backs away from politics is leaving his government to highly organized interest groups. He is contributing to a crisis in American politics that is moving the nation steadily toward an oligarchy—rule by the few.

Little about practical politics is taught in schools and colleges. In high schools, few teachers are equipped to teach more than a rudimentary course in civics; and this usually consists of the most general theory. While labor unions provide political instruction for their members, many business agencies, having established courses for their employees, then abandoned them as not worth the expense. The average white-collar worker and junior executive is too busy trying to make a living to pay much attention.

Those who do take an active interest in politics usually must dig out the information for themselves. Material is available from city and county clerks, election officials and secretaries of state around the country.

There are a few basic pieces of information that every citizen should have. He should know the names of his senators and representative in Congress; the names of the city councilman and county commissioner from his ward or district; the name of his local school board member; the name of the member of the legislature from his district; and that of the precinct or party spokesman from his area.

When an issue of vital importance arises, an interested citizen might write to these officials—or talk with any of them he knows. Most of them welcome intelligent, rational expression of opinion from the people whom they represent.

This does not mean that officials are anxious to get a mimeographed or form letter that has been proposed by some organization as part of a pressure campaign. They get too many of these. Unless an organization speaks for an important voting group in the home community, such mail has little influence.

If the correspondent is known to be active in political affairs, the letter will receive special attention. This is also true if he is known to give money, however little, to political campaigns, or if he writes with the authority of a community group. His organization might send a delegation to city hall, the county building, the state capital, even to

Washington, D.C., to present its views.

In rural communities 60 years ago, everyone took an active and willing part in local government. If a road needed repairs, farmers came out with teams and did the work themselves. If an education problem arose, people held a meeting at the schoolhouse to solve it.

Today, many do not know their neighbors, or want to. Even suburban families flee into high-rise apartments where they can sit and complain about government without finding out how to change things in a more complex society. Steadily, the responsibility for running the nation's affairs is being taken by fewer people.

Few want to do the political chores they are capable of doing. Most shy away from the necessary tasks like list-making from which they could gather experience. If they venture into politics at all, they want to go in at the top. According to one experienced politician:

> Amateur groups and committees for candidates want to organize the whole north side, or the west side, but you can't get them to take two precincts or one precinct and really concentrate on getting the names and going to see these people. The truth is that most of us don't like to go next door and ring that doorbell.

But amateurs can make a real difference in local affairs if they try. One man moved into a new community, joined his party's town committee and political club. The club sponsored various political activities with forums for speakers and the newcomer soon learned that his party needed a candidate for town supervisor. They were out-numbered by the other party four to one. No one wanted such a hopeless assignment. Traditionally, the candidate made one speech to the League of Women Voters and got out one piece of literature.

The newcomer announced his candidacy, knowing the odds but determined to do his best. He got money from people who had never given before. Making donations stimulated their interest. Advertisements endorsed by the principal of the local high school solicited support from political independents. A series of neighborhood parties brought people together in an informal atmosphere to meet the candidate. People began to know him. They discussed his views with their friends. Youngsters ran errands and distributed pamphlets.

After an exciting campaign, the newcomer lost. But when that office became vacant again, the dominant party was careful to select a candidate of stature and ability for the job, instead of a party hack. In addition, spokesmen for the minority were heard with new respect when they appeared before the city council meetings.

Not everyone, of course, is willing to offer himself as a personal sacrifice in order to improve his local community government. But a man with much practical political experience says:

> If you want to get the right people, get in and fight. Win or lose, you are going to gain. The more you do at the local level, the more influence you are going to have at higher levels. This is the only way to get the kind of people you want to run your party organization and your community.

The great changes in a community and in the nation usually come when a few people get angry about the way things are going.

One man, describing why he went into politics, said: "I got pretty mad at the party and I went out to save the world and fight the interests. I didn't know who they were or what they stood for but I was going to fight them anyway."

Anyone can look around and see that this one man did not save the world. But one person can start a chain reaction that forces the adoption of new policies.

In the 1930s, a gentle, kindly doctor, Francis Townsend, got the idea that every person over sixty should have a monthly pension. He mobilized elderly people and began a campaign. He was laughed at by the realists; his plan was called an illusion. At one point, gangsters tried to take over his movement to turn it into a racket. But the old man plodded on. In the end, the United States adopted a retirement plan that embraces many of Dr. Townsend's ideas.

• During World War II, the pay-as-you-go income tax plan came into being through the efforts of Beardsley Ruml.

• In 1949, the boss-controlled mayor of Grand Rapids, Michigan, was put out of power by a drive led by a grandmother.

• In a New Jersey community in the 1950s, a housewife, using the telephone, a station wagon and her neighbors, put on a drive that got a new library for her community.

• In the 1960s, the automobile industry and meat packers were compelled to adopt new safety standards by the pressures of Ralph Nader, a young lawyer.

Politicians regard fifteen or twenty persons as constituting a faction. If they are in the same neighborhood and are articulate, if they write letters to the editor or are prepared to sign a petition for a candidate, they can start the ball rolling. Inevitably, they will develop leadership. For example:

Sixty years ago, a New England doctor took a deep interest in public affairs. When problems developed, he invited his neighbors in to talk about them. When the doctor died, his daughter continued the discussion group. New residents were invited to join. The handful of neighbors have remained a strong, articulate and vital influence in the community. On local issues, they ask public officials for information and it is sent to them. Only about thirty persons are in the group, but if they get excited about something, they can muster as many as 600 votes. This is a faction.

Except for one brief interlude, Federalists, Whigs, and Republicans ran the town of Fairfield, Connecticut, from 1789 until 1959. The Democratic party was led by people who did not care enough about winning to put up good candidates.

Then five of the fifty-nine members on the Democratic town committee got together for coffee in a diner.

Talk turned to fighting the organization in the primary. Plans were developed secretly. The district was canvassed, house by house. Three of every four Democrats voted in the primary. The old-guard organization was swept out. The newly-organized party managed to elect two state representatives and a probate judge. Next, in the primary they defeated a Democratic judge who stood with the old-guard wing of the party. Then came the big drive to take over the town. It succeeded. It all began with five men.

There was a time when Seattle was run by the police department. Arthur B. Langlie, a former governor of Washington, said that in those days the only thing settled in elections was which part of the police department would collect the graft and which would be sent to outlying precincts. Finally, seventy-five young men got tired of the situation. They managed to elect a man to the city council. The young man fought vainly in the council. He was not allowed to investigate, could not get funds. But he did get some publicity.

Through this, people became convinced that the young man was right. Three new council members were elected to help him. Then came a reform mayor. The city got a police training school, a good fire department, transportation, new parks, paved streets, new bridges. People had begun to take their citizenship seriously.

In Portland, Oregon, Mrs. Dorothy Lee went into politics in the 1920s at the precinct level. In 1948, she was elected mayor. Within three years, she cleaned up the city, drove out the gamblers, closed brothels and developed an honest police force.

However much politicians are obligated to the men who put up money for their election, they must strike some compromise between the demands of their backers and those of the voting majority in their districts. To spurn the convictions of a watchful constituency would be political suicide. Hence, one convincing argument made by politicians to the money men in the background is that a friend in office voting for them when he can is better than an enemy fighting them on every issue.

It takes relatively few votes to change things, even in our complex, technical world. A set of figures, revised to fit the 1970 elections, provides this picture:

• In every election district seventy-four of each hundred adults are registered voters.

• Of these seventy-four, only fifty-five will vote on election day.

• Of the fifty-five, only twenty-one will vote in the primaries when candidates are chosen. This is an average of fewer than eleven in each party.

• Of those eleven, a candidate needs only six to win a primary.

These figures indicate that a dedicated six percent at work in each congressional district can control the country, and they illustrate how few would be needed to change the entire tone of American government. They can represent a profound hope for those interested in good government, or an ever-present danger to the lethargic citizen who sleeps through elections.

In Russia, only about five percent of the people are allowed to be members of the Communist party. By contrast, virtually every adult American has the privilege of belonging to a political party and voting as he pleases.

Yet, in America only about 2 out of 3 vote in the most important elections. Only 3 of each 100 take an active party interest, and about 1 of each 100 actually makes the major party decisions.

When a citizen in the United States disagrees with a governmental decision, he usually says: "They did it." It is always outrageous when "they" are doing something to "us." But in Germany, after the fall of Hitler, reflective people were heard to say: "I should have spoken out and I did not." They had learned what they needed to know about passing the buck.

CHAPTER FOURTEEN / **Trends for the Seventies**

It is apparent at the outset of the 1970s that the new decade will be filled with great danger and great opportunity. The political map of the United States is undergoing some fundamental changes. These represent a threat to one or the other of the two major political parties. They also carry with them new chances for new men both within and without the established parties to make their mark on the history of this country.

The changes which are taking place may be attributed to a number of factors:

— to population shifts, caused by flight to the suburbs from crime-ridden, drug-infested, polluted "central cities."

— to an enlarged middle class, spreading over the suburbs and converting itself to suburban social attitudes.

— to repercussions both in the North and the South caused by extension of civil rights to Negro citizens, including the right to vote.

— to new generations of young people who are questioning and challenging the policies, principles, and premises of the two major parties which compose the political "establishment" of the United States.

— to the relatively new electronic medium of communication—namely, television.

Some of these changes began to appear in the presidential election of 1968. The victory of the Republican candidate, Richard Nixon, was attributed to the majority he received in the combination of suburbs, small towns, and rural areas. This, together with the collapse of Democratic positions in the South, was more than enough to overcome the majority of Democrats in their traditional strongholds of the great cities of the country.

A Republican National Committee study of thirty-five major metropolitan areas showed that Mr. Nixon outran Hubert Humphrey in the suburbs by 8.4 million to 7.2 million votes. Mr. Humphrey ran one percentage point ahead in small cities, 11 percent ahead in cities of 50,000-500,000 population, and 25 percent ahead in cities of more than 500,000. However, the city vote in favor of the Democratic candidate was not decisive because Mr. Nixon scored an 11 percent lead in the suburbs, small towns, and rural areas, which, together, accounted for 71 percent of the voters in the 1968 election.

Herein lies a basic pattern for the 1970s—one which is encouraging Republicans to aspire to increasing power at national, state, and local levels. At the same time, it is confronting the Democrats with a critical challenge to their recent position as the dominant political force in the country.

The demographic and political map of the nation is changing under the dual pressures of adversity and affluence. The negative factors of crime and blight provide powerful reasons for leaving the city. The increasing incomes of blue collar workers and those of the lower middle class have enabled them to do so and to emigrate to the suburbs, previously the domain of upper income groups. A suburban home has now become a status symbol as well as a refuge for a steadily increasing number of people, cutting across previously stratified income and social lines.

A Louis Harris poll disclosed that 95 percent of Americans today consider a home "with green grass and trees around" to be a most important goal. Only 32 percent listed "enjoying the best in cultural experiences," the traditional appeal of city living, as equally important to their happiness. This attitude is reflected in census figures, which show that between 1960 and 1968 the suburban population rose from 31 to 35 percent while inner-city population declined from 32 to 29 percent.

This shift produced two important changes—one political, the other economic. When workers of the city moved out to join bankers and corporation executives in the suburbs, their thinking appears to have undergone a suburban coloration. Having acquired property in the form of a house and other earthly possessions which go along with it, the new suburbanites simultaneously acquired a strong interest in conserving their material goods and in holding taxes down so that the state would not be eating too much of the fruit of their labor. In other words, they began to turn away from the free spending policies of the Democratic party, with its expressed concern for the underdog, with whom they no longer identified themselves. They turned toward the more restrained principles of the Republican party, which might be expected to be mindful of the interests of the middle class and others who had acquired something they wanted to conserve.

For more than three decades, except for the Eisenhower years, the Democratic party had been sure of a good 70 percent of the labor vote. In 1968 the Democratic candidate for president received only 56 percent of the labor vote. That was a disaster for Mr. Humphrey, and it will continue to be one for the Democratic party if this trend should persist.

The slump of the Democratic vote in the ranks of labor coincided with the intensified flight from the cities. By 1968 about half of all trade union members, including 75 percent of those under age forty, had joined the more affluent members of society in the suburbs. Thus, while traditional Democratic strongholds were being undermined in the cities, many of their components were reappearing in the suburbs, transformed into Republican voters.

The economic consequences of the population shift were also striking. Business and industry accompanied their workers in the flight from the city. The new factories, shopping centers, high-rise apartments, and office buildings which continue to spring up in the booming suburbs represent a transfer of manufacturing, merchandising, management, and other economic activity from the central cities. As a result, cities are losing large taxpayers, both corporate and individual. While their sources of income are shrinking, their costs continue to soar under the combined impact of inflation, influx of needy Negroes from the South dependent on public welfare, rising crime and drug addiction. The widening gap between income and the cost of maintaining elementary services is one of the basic factors in the decay of our cities, described by President Nixon as "the most conspicuous failure in American life today."

The Rise of the Suburbs

(Residents as percent of total population)

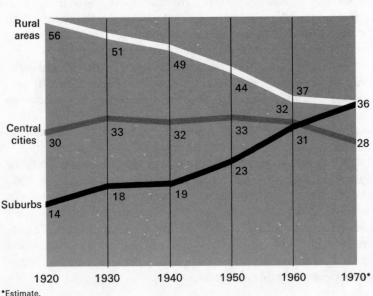

	1920	1930	1940	1950	1960	1970*
Rural areas	56	51	49	44	37	36
Central cities	30	33	32	33	31	28
Suburbs	14	18	19	23	32	36

*Estimate.

Source: U.S. Census Bureau

Ironically, the evils of the city from which business and the working middle class have fled are following them to the suburbs. Crime, pollution, and poverty do not stop at city limits and do not respect suburban signposts. Together with congested highways and crippled public transportation services, they are blossoming into major crisis situations affecting and threatening the entire metropolitan area. What this means is that the suburbanites, however much they would like to do so, cannot divorce themselves from the city. They and others much farther away, through taxes paid to the federal government, will have to face up to the problem of sustaining the financially failing cities.

Various proposals have been made to help solve city and metropolitan crises. Federal block grants to cities, or states and cities, are suggested. Federal or federal-state assumption of welfare costs, or of education or health burdens, is advanced. These are costly obligations.

Another proposal is to organize a consolidated government for city and suburbs, or at least a kind of federated metropolitan authority to cover certain functions of government. Some metropolitan areas already have taken steps in this direction.

Still other suggestions look toward incentives to keep the rural poor from pouring into big cities. Consideration is being given to new, small planned cities. Better transportation could take some of the city workers to jobs in the suburbs. More housing in the suburbs for low income people also is being promoted.

As the suburbs are brought closer to the cities by the need for a joint attack on common problems, the Democrats hope to build a bridge between their urban citadels and the suburban outcroppings, hoping thereby to recapture the affluent laborers and others who have wandered into the "enemy" camp. Their chances, of course, will depend on their success in producing programs and men offering greater promise than those of the Republicans for dealing with "the most conspicuous failure in American life today."

However, the Republicans and their presidential leader,

having focused on this problem, appear to be fully alive to the dangers and opportunities involved in the metropolitan crisis. A staff report by the Senate Republican Policy Committee, predicting that the population increase in metropolitan areas over the next twenty years would be greater than the total urban population of 1940, went on to say:

> The metropolitan issues will not disappear. They will only intensify. If they look impossibly complicated today, and we fail to do something about them, they will look worse next year. We cannot turn away from them. If a political party wishes to stay in the game of politics, it must tackle the public problems affecting the most persons. And those problems today and tomorrow are centered in the American metropolis.

The development of the trade union movement and its close association with the Democratic party enabled them to break the Republican hold on the Northeast and the Middle West so as to permit two-party politics to operate there. This historical process now appears to have a counterpart in the South, where the monopoly hold of the Democrats has been cracked and the way has been opened for the extension of the two-party system.

The results of the 1968 presidential election also serve to show what has happened to the "Solid South." Of the eleven states of the Confederacy, ruled by Democrats for nearly a century, Texas was the only one carried by Mr. Humphrey. The others were divided between Mr. Nixon and George Wallace, the candidate of the American Independent party.

This resounding setback for the Democrats was attributed to an emotional reaction against extension of civil rights to Negro citizens, for which southerners held a Democratic administration largely responsible, even though civil rights legislation had been endorsed by both major parties and the order to desegregate the schools had been handed down by a chief justice who was a Republican.

The Changing Map in the South

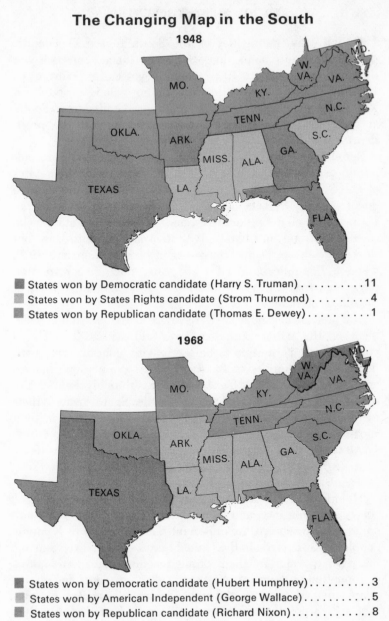

1948

■ States won by Democratic candidate (Harry S. Truman) 11
■ States won by States Rights candidate (Strom Thurmond) 4
■ States won by Republican candidate (Thomas E. Dewey) 1

1968

■ States won by Democratic candidate (Hubert Humphrey) 3
■ States won by American Independent (George Wallace) 5
■ States won by Republican candidate (Richard Nixon) 8

Source: USN&WR.

Actually, the strong ties of the South to the Democratic party have been coming loose for some time. Tennessee was the first to desert in 1920 when it voted for Warren G. Harding. Arkansas was the last to go when it voted for Mr. Wallace in 1968. Every state in the Confederate South, at one time or another, has now voted against the presidential candidate of the Democratic party.

Republican gains in the South have extended into adjacent, usually Democratic border states. In the sixteen states of the South and adjacent regions, Republicans now hold 6 governorships, 8 seats in the U. S. Senate, 36 seats in the U. S. House of Representatives, and 477 seats in state legislatures. The trend to a two-party system in the South was considered to have been firmly established in January, 1970, when a Republican, for the first time since Reconstruction days, took over the governor's office in Richmond, capital of the old Confederacy.

Full enfranchisement of the Negro introduces a new element at the ballot box. Just how and where the "Negro vote" will go, if there is to be a relatively cohesive vote, will depend on a number of factors, such as population changes and the appeals made by rival parties. Roughly half of the nation's 22 million Negroes live in the South, where their median income is estimated at 54 percent of the white median income. In view of the fact that it is 75 percent in the North Central states and 80 percent in the Western states, it is likely that Negroes will continue to emigrate from the South to those more attractive income areas.

In addition to population shifts there is the factor of new voters as young men and women reach voting age. The campaign of 1968 showed the important political role which young people have acquired in the United States even before securing the right to vote. By their strong reaction against unlimited continuation of the war in Vietnam, college students and young people helped produce the phenomenon of Senator Eugene McCarthy's political movement and touched off the campaign that, some said, spoiled President Johnson's hopes of remaining in the White House for another term.

The phenomenon of college students—and even high school students—taking an active part in political campaigns is new in the United States. It is still too early to see whether young people will move toward the traditional parties and seek to reform them from within or whether they will gravitate toward loosely organized or disorganized minority movements which will have some impact on the course of events from outside the established parties.

Kingman Brewster, president of Yale University, speaking of college students, said: "I think that what we do to them and for them during this coming decade is going to have probably more to do with what kind of country we end up with than anything else."

Neither of the two major parties appears to hold much attraction for college students, and neither is given high marks either for effort or for achievement. The voting age is still 21 in every state with four exceptions mentioned earlier: Georgia, Kentucky, Alaska, and Hawaii. Governor Nelson Rockefeller has declared himself in favor of lowering the voting age to 18. "Clearly," he said, "today's 18-year-olds are educated, responsible, and mature. Beyond that they show a deep concern for, and understanding of, the contemporary problems of America." Ohio and New Jersey voters recently rejected proposals to lower the voting age.

Whether or not the voting age is lowered, the activity of young people on and off the college campus is likely to produce political repercussions. Though they may not vote, they can raise their voices, they can demonstrate, and they can propagate viewpoints which could have an effect on those who do have the vote. The existence of independent, vocal individuals and groups, responsible to no one and completely free to say what they please, is something which may not be altogether to the liking of either of the established political parties. Yet, by needling the two parties, they may perform the service of keeping political leaders on their toes. By focusing on basic social and economic problems, they may con-

What Politicians Spent on
TV and Radio in Each State
(1968)

State	Amount	State	Amount
Alabama	$ 453,479	Montana	317,394
Alaska	355,576	Nebraska	314,648
Arizona	447,533	Nevada	361,122
Arkansas	986,186	New Hampshire	161,293
California	5,031,098	New Jersey	238,324
Colorado	350,749	New Mexico	312,576
Connecticut	333,754	New York	3,873,897
Delaware	97,252	North Carolina	1,125,194
Dist. of Col.	426,655	North Dakota	304,847
Florida	2,335,108	Ohio	2,731,266
Georgia	866,731	Oklahoma	670,013
Hawaii	554,630	Oregon	1,189,518
Idaho	141,906	Pennsylvania	2,119,664
Illinois	2,764,792	Rhode Island	414,307
Indiana	1,607,948	South Carolina	601,435
Iowa	771,687	South Dakota	222,837
Kansas	589,375	Tennessee	1,746,689
Kentucky	411,730	Texas	3,576,206
Louisiana	884,285	Utah	253,358
Maine	169,863	Vermont	69,334
Maryland	467,427	Virginia	299,132
Massachusetts	599,725	Washington	675,039
Michigan	1,143,682	West Virginia	661,181
Minnesota	447,101	Wisconsin	2,280,879
Mississippi	63,209	Wyoming	73,341
Missouri	2,420,363	**TOTAL**	**$49,315,338**

Additional spending for network television
and radio............................... 9,572,763

Overall total for radio and television **$58,888,100**

Note: Covers both primaries and general elections.
Source: Federal Communications Commission.

tribute to sustaining or intensifying pressure for solutions.

Independent and irreverent voices have acquired strength partly because television and radio have amplified them and partly because such paramount contemporary issues as war, inflation, pollution, crime, education, drugs, civil rights, and poverty are breaking the bonds of party loyalty. Television has also heightened the impact of these issues on the public mind by carrying them directly into the homes of voters. It is not so easy to dodge the issue of poverty or discrimination when viewers are confronted with the faces of victims on their television screens.

The importance of television as an instrument of political warfare is now generally recognized. According to a highly qualified expert, "I don't think any man will be elected to major office again—including mayors of large cities—without going on television to do it. And, therefore, it seems to me television will play a critical role in the future of politics and

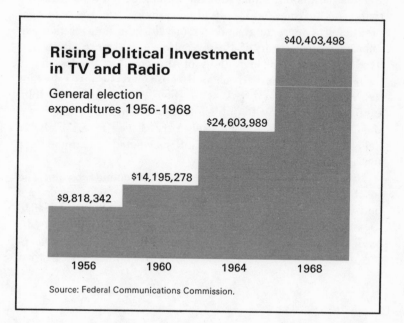

Rising Political Investment in TV and Radio

General election expenditures 1956-1968

$40,403,498

$24,603,989

$14,195,278

$9,818,342

1956   1960   1964   1968

Source: Federal Communications Commission.

the future of our lives." The statement was made by Roger E. Ailes, who is credited with having played a key role in winning the presidency for Mr. Nixon by the way he presented the Republican candidate to the public through the paid television programs he produced.

Senator John Pastore of Rhode Island agrees that television is indispensable for a political candidate, but he finds the cost "appalling." He said that a candidate may have to spend $2 million on television to win a Senate seat paying $42,500 a year. This raises the unresolved problem of a conflict between the duty of a successful candidate to serve the public and his obligation to the individuals who put up the money essential for his election. This issue is sure to agitate the public and the Congress as various proposals are advanced to make the public airways, now exploited commercially by private companies, available to political candidates at reduced cost or no cost at all.

Thus paramount issues and the impact of television, dramatizing both issues and individuals, may have the effect of producing a more fluid and a more flexible state of political affairs in the decade of the seventies. Fixed party lines and fixed loyalties in fixed regions of the country are less likely to hold. Individuals with a good cause may be less reluctant to defy or even to break with their party machines. John Lindsay, rejected by Republicans, ran as an independent and was reelected mayor of New York City. Peter Flaherty defied the Democratic machine and succeeded in being elected mayor of Pittsburgh.

This points to the importance of the independent voter and to the "silent, sleeping majority"—the millions who do not bother to vote. In the 1968 election the number who failed to vote, 47 million, exceeded the number, 31 million, who made Richard Nixon president. A small fraction of these sleeping millions could change the course of politics and history.

Index